I0192571

All characters, places or events portrayed in this book are accurate to the best of the authors knowledge and any disagreement with this portrayal will be taken under advisement.

Publication Date: May 2014
Print ISBN 978-1-938586-61-3
eBook ISBN 978-1-938586-62-0

Printed in the United States of America
Writers Cramp Publishing
http://www.writerscramp.us/
editor@writerscramp.us

Mom and Dad and Mike

This book is dedicated to my children, grand children, great grand children and all to follow. I want to thank my loving wife of 56 years for her unwavering dedication, determination and encouragement as we put together this book.
We did it Honey!

Steven Keith Clark

Table of Contents

THE PATH WELL TAKEN

THE REST OF MY STORY:

Clark Family Tree

Father
Steven Keith Clark

Mother
Helen Louise Clark

Children

- Pamela Clark (Jeff Spitzer)
- Tim Clark (Stacy)
- Dwight Clark (Michelle)
- Rod Clark (Deborah)

Grand Children

- Kyle (Mallory) Spitzer
- Eli Spitzer
- Colin Moore
- Quentin Moore
- Kayla
- Taylor
- Seth
- Heidi Cook
- Kimbra (Matt Birchler)
- Jeff
- Anna (John O'Brien)
- Levi
- Katie (Harvey Fryberger)

Great Grand Kids

- Allie
- Cora
- Mark
- Emma
- Abigail
- Clara
- Alice
- Patrick
- Jackson
- Charlie
- Silas
- Violet

The Path Well Taken

Introduction

This is a story about a baby boy who was in an orphanage in Denver, Colorado and was adopted by Dwight and Bernice Clark, a man and wife from the southeastern plains near Lamar, Colorado. It tells of his years growing up in Prowers and Kiowa County and the life he built.

There are stories told in here that are true and remembered by the author. Others have been passed down from friends and relatives and believed to be true and factual. Some will make you laugh and others might make you shed tears. Some will scare you, as you will notice the guardian angels were really busy at times.

All people mentioned or talked about in this book are real and there will be a summary on some as to their past and why they play an important role in this book.

So many stories told to me as a child when television and radio were not in our home were stories that not only entertained me, but were also history of the Clarks' and Bentleys'. This will be told in various stages in words to follow.

It is the author's belief that a friendly smile will make you many new friends, and will keep friends you already have. A quote from Granddad Clark was 'always have a happy thought and you will live a long life'.

Chapter One

The year was 1936. It was July 3rd, a hot and dry day. The dust bowl days of the 1930's was still pushing its vengeance on the plains of the western states. The depression had crippled people who earlier had thought they would never see times as they were experiencing.

Dwight and Bernice Clark had been married over six years and had no children. They decided on adoption. Along with Bernice's Uncle Ray Bentley and his wife, Ella, they traveled by bus to Denver to an orphanage to hopefully adopt a baby girl.

At the orphanage they were given the opportunity to see children ranging in age from babies to teenagers needing a home. They were walking past the children and hopefully would choose a baby girl.

As they were walking thru the orphanage that morning, some of the older children were saying 'take me, take me'. They wanted a home. But Dwight and Bernice were looking for a young baby. They kept looking at babies. One looked at them with just a big 'smile'. Dwight immediately said 'there's the one I want'. It was a boy, not a girl. He was three months and three days old, just right. The smile is what stole Dwight's heart. He said, 'he's the one'.

After doing paperwork they were released with the baby to go back to Lamar, Colorado with the possible chance to adopt at a later date.

The bus had no air conditioning and the trip back to Lamar

Dwight and Bernice Clark (Mom and Dad)

was a long ride, but they were excited, having a baby they had so much wanted for years.

Dwight was 38 years old and Bernice was 32 years old. It was time for a family even if times were hard with the drought still on and jobs were not very easy to find.

After the bus arrived in Lamar, they took their baby home to Clay Creek Store that Dwight and Bernice had purchased from Joe Hawkins, who became part of the family some years later.

On arrival to the store located on Highway 287 between Lamar and Springfield, they were greeted by Steve and Eva Clark. After a time of cuddling and making over the baby, the Clark grandparents asked what they had named the baby. The answer was 'we did not have a name picked out for a boy'. Steve Clark replied 'why not name him Steven Keith Clark'? You see, his first name was Stephanus and his mother's maiden name was Keith. Therefore, Steven Keith Clark had a name after his Granddad and great grandmother Keith.

From here on Dwight and Bernice Clark will be referred to as Dad and Mom. Steven Keith Clark was called Keith instead of Steven, probably because of there already being a Granddad Steve.

The grandparents on the Clark side of Keith moved to Colorado from Chautauqua County Kansas in 1916. They homesteaded southwest of Lamar. They had five sons and three daughters. Dwight was the oldest of their children. He was a Junior in high school when he came to Colorado. Upon graduation from high school in 1918, he homesteaded 30 miles southwest of Lamar. His homestead was about six miles south of his parents homestead. His house consisted of a building about

12' by 15' that he lived in. It was wood frame with tarpaper covering the wood.

Dad and his brother, Fred were both injured quite seriously when they were grade school boys at ages nine and seven. The story goes that on Christmas Eve about 1907, the boys went hunting with friends near their home in Chautauqua County Kansas. Their dog dug up a package near a tombstone in a cemetery. Dad picked it up to look at it while the other boys stood by and watched. It exploded in Dad's hand. It was nitroglycerin that had been left behind from a well drilling operation. It had been covered up with dirt when his dog uncovered it.

The explosion took most of Dad's right hand off and destroyed his sight in one eye. It also damaged one of Uncle Fred's eyes and made a hole in his side. With the help of the neighbor boys they were able to get home. Granddad Clark went to town and brought a Doctor back with him. The Doctor had to cut off the rest of Dad's mangled right hand. He also dressed Uncle Fred's wound. They were afraid he would get infection and die. Dad lost the rest of the school year but was able to return to school the next year.

Dad played softball in grade school with his classmates. One story he told was after hitting the ball and running the bases he collided with a car that was coming up a rut road through the ball field. It knocked him out for a while. When he woke up the first thing he remembered was opening his eyes and seeing his classmates all standing over him. The first thing he did was reach in his shirt pocket for his raisins he quite often carried. They knew he was all right then.

While attending high school in Caney, Kansas, he was on the

football and track team. After moving to Colorado he continued with these two sports. He graduated from Lamar Union High School in Lamar, Colorado at the age of 20 in 1918.

When Dad lost his hand in 1907, the drilling company responsible for the explosives awarded him Three Thousand Dollars payable to him when he turned Twenty One years old.

He used this money to purchase livestock and this was the beginning of ranching operation.

Dad was a true cowboy. He would stay at his parents homestead during school months after his graduation so the younger brothers and sisters could live in Lamar in a rented house with their parents and attend grade school and high school. All the boys were active in football and track.

A Great Uncle to Eva Clark, Wes Bassore, also homesteaded directly north of Steve Clark's homestead. It made it possible for him to live in his small house but to walk the short distance to the Clark home for his meals. He was a Civil War Veteran and never married. He is buried in the Fairmount Cemetery in Lamar next to the Clark grandparents. He died in 1928 at the age of 90.

Dad continued to live this life on his homestead. He was a lifelong friend of the Hasser brothers Aaron and Oscar, who lived close by in the rough grasslands in the edge of the Cedars close to his homestead.

Dad, Aaron and Oscar attended a dance close to Deora, Colorado, south of Las Animas. He looked out on the dance floor and spotted Bernice Keeler and told Oscar "there's the gal I'm gonna marry!" He had never seen her before. She was a school teacher at Rock Crossing School near Deora. They

Mom and Dad on their wedding day

courted and were married in the Methodist Church in Lamar on June 16, 1930.

Mom was born in Fayetteville, Arkansas on December 7, 1904. Her parents were Maude Bentley Keeler and Ed Keeler. Four years later a sister, Edna was born and Maude died in childbirth. Ed Keeler died a year later leaving a baby and a four year old to be raised by family members. Maude's mother, Addie Bentley, raised her granddaughter, Bernice and actually adopted her. Mom kept her name Keeler instead of changing it to Bentley.

Edna was taken in and raised by the Keeler family and soon moved to Wyoming in the Rock Springs area at Farson, Wyoming. The sisters never saw each other again until they were grown girls. They corresponded with one another often.

In 1914 the Grandmother Bentley, who was widowed by this time, came to Colorado and homesteaded about 36 miles south of Las Animas. She was accompanied to Colorado by her young granddaughter, Bernice, and her two youngest sons, Frank and Earl.

This was about fifteen to twenty miles on southwest of where Dad homesteaded. Grandmother Bentley, Frank, and Earl all homesteaded close to each other. Mom attended school at Rock Crossing and boarded out in Springfield to attend high school. She graduated from high school in 1922.

After graduation Mom moved to Montana where her mother, Maude, had a sister, Fern Bentley living and teaching on an Indian Reservation. Mom attended Normal School for a year and received a teaching certificate. Mom was able to visit her sister, Edna, on the trip to Montana and probably on the return trip to Baca County, Colorado.

Edna was living near Farson, Wyoming and still in school at this time. Her foster dad, Bert Keeler, was a rancher and also a State Senator for some time in Wyoming.

When Mom returned to Colorado she obtained a teaching job at Rock Crossing School. It was not far from where she was raised and would either ride a horse or walk to school. Her nephew, Frank Bentley's son, Albert, had started school and went with her. He was a student of hers. At this time it was in the late 1920's.

The house where Mom was raised was made out of rock. It had a flat roof that was covered with sod. There was a hand dug well, several hundred yards downhill from the house by a creek that only ran live water after a rain. Water was carried by buckets uphill to the house. Frank and Earl built this house and hand dug the well for their mother.

After Dad and Mom were married, she got a teaching job at a one room school called Hopewell. Dad and Mom were living in a house on Cat Creek at this time that he had purchased some years earlier.

Dad, by this time, had a large herd of cattle and had leased or bought more land with his success in the livestock business.

In the next few years the drought and depression had a big grip on everyone. Dad was able to hang on for a few years and even shipped cattle to the flint hills in Kansas with Oscar and Aaron Hasser. Earlier when he had shipped cattle to market, he drove them to Lamar and shipped them by rail to Kansas City and rode the train along with the cattle. He told of sitting with a man and visiting and found out he was A. L. Duckwall. Mr.

Grandparents Steve and Eva Clark

Duckwall told Dad he had been very successful financially but there were a lot of health problems in his family.

After the sale of his cattle in Kansas City, Dad took the train up to Northern Missouri where his Dad, My Granddad Steve, grew up. Dad had six uncles and an aunt still living there as well as his grandmother, Angeline Keith Clark. It was good that Dad did this because the family had been apart for many years because of an incident that happened when my Granddad Steve was about fourteen years old.

The story goes that my Granddad Steve and his older brother, Abraham, sixteen years old, decided to make a small canon. They took a metal bedstead apart and cut it to make a gun barrel. They put gun powder in the barrel and packed it with some sort of projectile. They went out to the pasture where the cattle were and set it off, hitting the herd bull. The bull fell down. They thought they had killed it so they decided they best leave the country. Their Dad, Abraham, a Civil War veteran was known to have quite a temper!

The two young boys headed west. Midway into Kansas, the brothers split up. Abraham told Steve he might go on toward Washington or stay in Kansas. Granddad went on out to Cripple Creek, Colorado and never heard from his older brother again.

After a short time in Cripple Creek during the Gold Rush days, Granddad witnessed a couple of fights where men were killed. He decided to head back East and get out of the Wild West!

He eventually wound up in southeast Kansas and started working in the oil fields as a driller. This is where he met my Grandmother, Eva Harris Clark. They were married in Sedan,

Kansas. All but two of their children were born there. Glen was born in Indian Territory, which was Bartlesville, Oklahoma, after it became a state.

Granddad ran a livery stable in Bartlesville for a while. Marjorie, who was twenty years younger than Dad, was born in Lamar after they moved to Colorado.

Granddad used to tell my Grandma that he had no family. After much persistence, she finally was told what he had done as a fourteen year old. Grandma connected with the family by correspondence. Granddad, a few years later, went back to Missouri and reunited with his younger siblings and his mother. His Father, Abraham, was deceased by then and his mother Angeline was blind. The family never again heard from the oldest son, Abraham, who with Steve had run away from home in the year 1884.

One brother of Granddad's, Uncle Charlie came to southeast Kansas and stayed with Granddad and Grandma for a while. He met and married his mate, Aunt Nellie, while living in Kansas. The two later returned to Northern Missouri and lived there the rest of their lives. They never had any children.

Dad told of a time when he traveled by train to northern Missouri that was pretty amusing. He was staying with Granddad Steve's brother, Uncle Dwight. Dad was told there was a dance over the hill from Uncle Dwight's house and a lot of Dad's first cousins would be there. Dad wanted to go because he loved to dance and he also wanted to become better acquainted with his cousins. Uncle Dwight brought out a saddle horse for Dad to ride. He had the horse saddled up and one stirrup was missing, but there was a corn planter plate in place of it. He told Dad that the horse would buck once in a while, but that shouldn't bother him, being a cowboy from Colorado! Dad told me he was a little nervous after seeing the planter plate and hearing of occasional bucking, but he was not going to say anything. He mounted the horse and rode off with never a bucking moment!

Dad had to find outside work during the 1930's as grass was not available for his cattle and he had to down size his herd. My parents eventually lost most of their acquired land and the leased land and sold what cattle was left.

Dad got work with the Worker's Progress Administration (WPA) where his brother, Clifford, was a foreman on the bridge crew for WPA). One of his bridges is still in use across Cat Creek southwest of Lamar. Uncle Cliff's name is engraved on the double archway of this bridge.

Dad bought cattle for the Government to ship to slaughter houses when there was no more feed available to feed the cattle. The ranchers were paid by the government for the cattle shipped. If the cattle were too weak to be shipped, they were shot and buried. The government used the processed cattle to help feed the starving people. The ranchers were paid approximately $18.00 per cow and less for calves. They didn't pay as much for the ones that had to be destroyed.

Dad and Mom later purchased the Clay Creek Store, a grocery store and gas station as was mentioned earlier when I joined the family.

They used to tell me about gypsies traveling in groups. The gypsies would all converge at once at the store and you had to watch them closely. They would get Dad outside to fill their vehicles with gas and others would gather up food inside the

Uncle Ray and Aunt Ella Bentley

store. If one was not careful and keep a close eye on them, they would fill their pockets with merchandise or even try to sneak into the cash drawer. The cash drawer was usually a muffin tin for coins and a cigar box for paper money.

The gas pump was a hand operated pump handle that was moved back and forth to raise gas up into a glass bowl above the pump. It would be marked in gallons with lines to indicate how much gas was drained out by gravity flow.

The Clay Creek Store was located about fifteen miles from Hopewell School so Mother did not teach there again after they purchased the store. Mother was able to obtain another teaching job at a school close to the store. It was a one room school about three miles west of the store. This was near the Shear homestead. She had in her classroom Albert, Irene, Lucy, Vera, John and Betty Shear. This was a lot closer to the store but still cars were slow and the roads were just trails. She had a chance to trade schools with another teacher, Dorothy Smith, who later married Dad's younger brother, Ralph. Aunt Dorothy's school, Sunnyslope, was closer yet to the store on Clay Creek. The trade was good for them both as Aunt Dorothy was single and able to board with the Shear family.

Mom used to laugh and tell the story of a day when she was sick and sent Dad to school to fill in as the teacher. Dad was writing a health lesson on the blackboard. One statement he wrote on the board was "DO NOT SMOKE" all the while he had a cigarette fired up. One of the students told on him when Mom returned the next day. Got caught, didn't he?

Dad purchased the second Model A Ford sold in Lamar. Orie Wood bought the first one. It was a 1928 Model A. Dad was a little rough on cars using them for hauling oil cake and other supplies as well as chasing coyotes, etc. He bought another new car in 1929 as he was still doing great in the cattle business. He took Mom to Fayetteville, Arkansas in this car on their honeymoon in 1930. After things got worse with the economy he was still using it in the mid 1930's. Mother had purchased a used Chevrolet. It was well taken care of and was not used in the pastures. One winter night a gentleman caught a ride to the store. He had run out of gas several miles from the store. He got Dad up in the middle of the night in a snowstorm to take him and some gas back to his vehicle. Dad took Mom's Chevrolet and did not see the other car until after they sideswiped one another. There went the good car. Now they had only the Model A to use. It would be years before they could purchase anything nicer.

Dad sold the store to his parents in 1937 and they operated it until 1953 when they sold it and moved into Lamar.

We moved to Cheyenne Wells in 1937 when I was one year old. Dad worked for WPA measuring land. It was during this time that Dad met Edward Smartt who was also working in land measurement. Ed had been in college studying for a degree to become an ASC worker. Dad became a good friend to the Smartt family, Ed's father, Hackett and his uncles included.

When I was married in 1958, Ed, his wife Josephine, and children Phil, Ken and Carol were at our wedding. I was a member of the First Baptist Church where the Smartt family was active. My wife, Louise, was a member of the First Christian Church where the Ausmus family was members. Monte Ausmus was nine years old when he attended our wedding with his parents. Carol Smartt was six years old. I am telling this part in my story here because Monte and Carol did not know one another. They were later married and moved to the country where they are neighbors a few miles to the west. Ken Smartt is also a neighbor.

I encouraged Monte to help me when I was working in the oil and gas field taking care of oil and gas wells for various companies as a contract pumper. Monte and I later purchased a stripper oil well. We have a great relationship in our ventures together.

I mention this part of my story ahead of time, because Monte and I do a lot of work together in the oil and gas business as well as farming and cattle.

Monte has been pushing me to write down stories I am always telling him. He tells me history needs to be recorded and to hurry up and do this! I also want my children, grandchildren and great grandchildren to know of their Clark heritage.

After a year living and working in Cheyenne Wells, it was back to Lamar to live. Dad worked various jobs again for the WPA. Most of this work was for one dollar per day. This was about 1938.

In 1939 we moved back on Cat Creek to the home Dad and Mom lived in when they were first married. Times were still tough with very little money in their pockets.

Dad obtained a loan from FSA which helped ranchers get back on their feet. He still had his homestead land along with some other land he had owned before the depression, but some he had to turn back to creditors.

Mr. Joe Compton, who was financially stable purchased about 40 head of cattle and let Dad take them to his pasture.

In return, the calf crop was split between Joe and Dad. After a numbers of years, according to their agreement, the cattle were all Dad's.

By the late 1930's the dust bowl days were diminishing. Rain was more abundant and the economy was improving. Many of the homesteaders had already returned to the east or left for California to work. This meant that the ones still here could lease land cheap and try to make a fresh start. By late 1939 and 1940, I can recall things that were happening as I was four years old then.

Dad was no longer working for WPA. He did, however, take a job of laying sod on the Lamar Football Field. The rock stadium had been built by WPA workers. This is located between south seventh and south ninth streets. Dad used his team of horses to plow up some buffalo grass on the land out south, and with his team and a wagon, hauled the grass to the stadium to seed the football field. I do not remember this but as I said, most of this book so far is stories I heard often. We would have company over for dinner frequently. While the women were cleaning up the dishes, the men would tell stories. I would listen and take it all in if there were not any children visiting to play with. We had no electricity or running water. That also meant no telephone or radio. This is how life was then.

We had a spring on Cat Creek that was about 300 yards from the house. Dad would carry two buckets at a time to the house with water.

One story in particular I remember being told was the time I was just a toddler walking good when I fell into a five gallon bucket about half full of waste water. I leaned over it and fell in head first. Dad just happened to look over and see my feet sticking out and quickly retrieved me. Maybe that was my Guardian Angel's first job with me!

In the late 1930's Dad wintered some cows over between Wiley and McClave. We stayed in a small house there by the leased pasture. When Dad and Mom went home on a week-end to check on things at Cat Creek, it seems as though thieves had taken most of their furniture, including Mom's Hope Chest. They had a tip on who might have stolen the furniture but were unable to convict them.

The Model A Ford the folks drove was pretty well worn out and had been parked in a junk pile. Too much abuse and blow dirt sucked into the motor, I guess. Granddad Clark was running the Clay Creek Store he had purchased from Dad. The store was never closed, open seven days a week. If someone knocked on the door in the middle of the night, Granddad would sell whatever was needed. He and Grandma never left the store so he loaned us the Model T Ford he didn't need. It was a 1926 Roadster with a cloth top on it at one time. The cloth was missing so it was a convertible with a windshield in front that helped break the wind.

I remember going from Cat Creek to the store after a snowstorm. It was about a twelve mile trip. The road had no gravel on it but it had been graded, leaving barrow pits on each side part of the way. It had warmed up enough that the snow was melting and the road was very muddy. This was not too much of a problem with a Model T or Model A as these cars had tall narrow wheels that would cut the snow and mud into deep ruts but would keep on going. The problem that day was that it was working the twenty horsepower motor in the Model T to the max. It started to boil the water in the radiator. Dad would shut the car off to let it cool and all the time was packing snow into the radiator to let it melt to replace the water that had boiled out. We would travel another mile or two then repeat the process until we finally made it to the store. Oh yes, there was no battery in this car and it was cranked each time it was started. The radiator was drained after use each night so that it would not freeze. Anti Freeze was not used. When we did make a trip into Lamar, which was no more than once a month in the winter, Mom would lay a blanket across our laps. The heat from the engine that came up through the floor kept us warm.

We bought most of our groceries from Granddad's store. We used to buy flour by the big sack, sugar in fifty pound bags and potatoes in one hundred pound bags. We also had lard in big buckets. We usually had milk in the condensed cans, so what else did one need? Popcorn was usually available most of the time.

The house at Cat Creek was a four room house with the chimney in the middle. There was a hen house and corrals, but no barn.

The house had a stove that used wood or coal and a three burner kerosene cookstove. Each burner on the cooking stove had a big round wick that could be raised by a knob to crank it up so the flame would put out more heat. It had a gallon glass jug on the end that was turned upside down. The kerosene filled the line and kept the wick wet for the fire.

Next to the house was a fruit cellar. It was always creepy to me because it was built out of cedar posts side by side and covered with tar paper and rounded off with dirt over the top. There were always spiders in there. Dad always looked closely for snakes before entering the cellar. The cellar was used not only for canned goods but also for extra storage as the house did not have a lot of storage space. The thing I remember most is that any time day or night that a storm would come up, we would head to the cellar because there might be a tornado. You see, Dad was about eighteen years old when his family moved from eastern Kansas. They had lots of tornados in Kansas, so he was worried that we might get in one here.

The Hasser brothers, Sniff Brothers and Clark Brothers (Dad and his brother Clifford) decided to build a dipping vat for their cattle. This consisted of a narrow trench about fifteen to twenty feet long and seven or eight feet deep. This was filled with water from the spring with a pump that was run by an old single cylinder engine. You put the medicine in the vat and drove the cattle through the vat to treat them for scabies, lice, etc. Before they had the vat at Cat Creek, the cattle had to be driven some distance north to the river country.

Our mail was delivered on the road in front of our house. Our mail carrier was from Lamar on Route 3. The mail was only delivered two or three times per week with the mail going south and east of Lamar on the other days. We were south and west of Lamar. Our mail carrier was Giles Strong. Mr. Strong always had a special spot in my life. He married Audrey Angell's sister-in-law. Audrey was the oldest of Dad's three sisters. Uncle Otis Angell was a brother to Ruth Strong. Uncle Otis started out with the Post Office in Springfield, Colorado and later transferred to Denver where he retired from the postal service.

The Strong's were not related to me but I always thought they were my cousins, too. All of our family gatherings on the Clark side always included them when the Angells came from Denver to visit. The Strong children included a son, Bob and daughters Mary and Virginia. Virginia is just a few years older than me. We were in high school together and have always been close friends (since she can't be MY cousin, too!) We have a lot in common with some of the same relatives.

A special time I remember while living at Cat Creek was a cold, snowy day and I could not be outside playing. There was a knock on the door and when the door was opened, there stood Mr. Strong with the mail. Also in his hand was a coloring book and a box of crayons for me. A small boy does not forget something like that. Neither did many of the other people on his route. When someone needed groceries, chicken feed, medicine, etc., Mr. Strong was a saint and will always be remembered by many. It was my privilege in later years to have the honor of delivering mail to him when I was a substitute mail carrier on his part of town.

Mr. and Mrs. Strong also played a very important role in my wife's younger years. The Strongs lived in the same block on North Eleventh Street as Louise and her family. He was very instrumental in getting the Bever family in the First Christian Church. Mr. Strong was a very active leader in his church work and a book could be written on that!

One afternoon in late February or early March in 1941, we went to Granddad's store to get some groceries and visit. While there a little storm came up and it rained with a lot of thunder and lightning. The folks decided that it would be a muddy trip back to the rancrh and we should stay the night and go home early the next morning. We had no cows to milk or other chores that could not wait. The chickens would go into their small hen house and roost. We had just acquired a new dog and Dad had put him in the empty chicken coup to make sure he did not leave until he was used to the place. I was excited about the new dog as he would be a playmate. He was about six months old. Our old dog, Jack, a German Shepherd, had gone with us to the store one day and had been run over by a truck. I remember one particular incident about Jack the short time we had him. Dad quite often made fudge. This particular day he made two platters, one with cocoa and one without. He set the two platters outside to cool and set up. When he went out later to bring the fudge in he said "we were going to be disappointed as the one without cocoa had been eaten by Jack".

We left the store about mid morning the next day for home. The roads were not too muddy. We were about one fourth mile from home when I heard my Mother start screaming "Dwight, Dwight, look, look!" Dad said "look at what?" Mom said "the house, the house, it's gone!" We drove up to the front where only the door step and some smoldering ashes were still smoking. Our house had burned completely down. Mom was crying and Dad was probably in shock. I was scared. Dad opened up the chicken coup to let the new dog out. The dog must have gotten pretty warm as he was about fifty feet from the house. He took off on a dead run on the prairie and we never saw him again.

When Mom could talk, she told Dad that she had left her diamond ring and wedding band on the dresser in the bedroom. I can still see this scene as if it happened yesterday. Dad picked up a stick and walked in the ashes and stirred them around for less than a minute. The sun made something glisten. It was Mom's diamond with a glob of melted gold with it. He had found her diamond.

I received a new tricycle for Christmas a few months before and no place to ride it but in the house. I did however, a few days earlier take it outside to ride on the hard ground and had left it outside. My tricycle was still where I had left it but it had been so hot from the fire that the rubber tires had burned off. I remember Mom going to different stores in Lamar to try to buy new tires, but was unable to ever get any.

We kept a few things in the storm cellar (fruit) that did not burn. One thing I remember was a pair of red and black boots that had once belonged to an older cousin, Jinx Clark. The boots were mine now, but I had to grow into them first. They were kept in the cellar but every few months I would ask Mom to let me see if they fit yet. They had been brought in the house for me to try on and they had been left in the house. They went up in flames!

It was never known for certain what caused the fire. Could have been lightning but someone said they had driven past the house that evening and thought they had seen a light on. There was no electricity of course. In this time and era it was not uncommon for a person travelling through to stop and find something to eat. If this had been the case and they forgot to turn the coal oil wick down after cooking a meal, it could have grown to a higher flame, catching the wallpaper on fire.

Chapter Two

It was back into the Model T and go to Granddad and Grandma's or to my Uncle Ray and Aunt Ella's home. They lived in a small house close to Clay Creek Store. It was about two city blocks north of the store.

At this time I need to explain the closeness of my life with Uncle Ray and Aunt Ella Bentley. Uncle Ray was an older brother of Mom's mother, Maude and Frank and Earl.

Uncle Ray had left Arkansas just ahead of Grandmother Bentley in about 1912 or 1913. He homesteaded in the Oklahoma panhandle. His wife Ella had also homesteaded on land that joined Uncle Ray. Aunt Ella's cat had wandered to his place one day and he returned the cat to its owner.

This started a courtship that eventually led to a marriage. They never had any children of their own but they were like grandparents to me and all of his nieces and nephews. Uncle Ray was the biggest tease to children I ever knew. He could talk to children on their level. I thought he could do anything and he loved us all so much.

Uncle Ray and Aunt Ella came to dinner at our house one time when I was around five years old. I did not have any brothers or sisters so I was used to entertaining myself, usually playing with a dog or cat. I was often digging holes in the ground. Uncle Ray asked me what I was doing. I told him I was digging a deep hole. He wanted to see it. It was probably three feet wide and eighteen inches deep. Uncle Ray said "if you keep digging you will soon be to China on the other side of the world and you will have a Chinese boy to play with." I dug on that hole day after day but I never did get to China!

Uncle Ray always had a Jersey milk cow and he fed her bran flakes. He gave me some to eat, too. They were good. There was always lots of milk and cream. Aunt Ella always had a garden with strawberries. That meant there was strawberry shortcake with whipped cream. I'm sure I had Uncle Ray wrapped around my little finger! They were so special to me. Uncle Ray died when I was twelve years old. He had an operation and bled to death on the operating table. He was sixty five years old.

Aunt Ella was still alive when my oldest son, Rod was a little boy. My wife, Louise and I ate many dinners with Aunt Ella after we were married. She lived in Lamar by then. We especially loved her apple waldorf salad.

My young mind was worried that we would have no place to live when we went back to the store after the fire to tell my grandparents what had happened. We stayed with them for about a month until we moved into a house that was empty about a mile from Cat Creek. It was known as the Ward place.

The day we moved in was on my Fifth birthday. What did we move in? Well a lot of neighbors and family and friends from Lamar showed up with chairs, beds, clothes, dishes and other necessities for a home. Mr. Skinner, a barber from Lamar, brought Dad a big stuffed chair.

The Ward house had a cistern and a rock outside toilet, but no barn or other out buildings. It was a bigger house than the one we lost to a fire. We had to haul water on the wagon pulled by the team of work horses, (Prince and Barney). Dad filled the barrels full of water taken from the spring at cat creek with a bucket and dumped it in the cistern.

There were no trees and no close neighbors where we lived. I would play in the shade of the house in the summer and indoors in the winter. I would go with Dad in the Model T to check cattle. Sometimes he used his saddle horse for checking cattle. If we used the work horses and wagon for jobs that required them, I would ride along.

Dad did farm a few acres planting mostly feed to help winter the cows. One year in 1942 he planted corn. It did well as there was substantial rain that summer.

I remember going out in the corn field in the late summer. I would have been six years old. Dad just walked out far enough to see how well the corn crop was doing. We came upon a prairie rattler. Dad did not have anything along to kill it. He told me to stay back. Dad pulled up a stalk of corn about four feet long. He used it to hit the snake until it was partially injured. All at once, Dad jumped in the middle of the action landing on the snake with his cowboy boot heel twisting on the snake while continuing to back out of the corn field.

Prince and Barney were great work horses. They were well trained and would stop and go on verbal command. They pulled the wagon while Dad would shuck the corn and toss it into the wagon.

The corn was stored in an empty house about a mile north of where we were living. It was known as the Pidge place.

The work horses were both large horses. Barney was a dark horse and Prince was a bay. Barney was a little bit on the lazy side, letting Prince pull more when it came to work. Dad had these horses long before I was born. They lived until the very late 1940's. They were probably over twenty years old.

The 1940's were much the same routine, the same thing over and over each year.

Oscar and Grace Hasser, along with their two children, Donna and Marvin, would often come to visit, or else we would go to their place. Grace and Mom were friends long before either were married. Grace was also a school teacher.

Marvin and I were always good friends from our early childhood to this day. Our families would go to Two Buttes Lake to camp out. The men would fish and Donna, Marvin and I would play. We often found horny toads in the rocks. We slept in a large tent, all together!

The Riley's lived about four miles from us. They always had a new car and would stop and take us to Lamar with them. This was quite a trip. Leroy Riley and his wife, Rose, had been neighbors to my Grandparents in Kansas. They all came to Colorado together to homestead. They shipped their cattle together when moving from Kansas to Colorado.

The Riley's had a granddaughter, Shirley Riley, who lived with them through high school. She also visited a lot of summers with her grandparents. I always considered her my first girlfriend, even though she was two years older than me. Age did not make much difference in those days. You were just happy to have someone to play with, boy or girl, younger or older.

Uncle Ralph, my Dad's youngest brother lived in Lamar and was the Standard Oil Bulk Agent when World War II had begun. Uncle Ralph was drafted into the army. Aunt Dorothy and the children, Floy, Glen and Sue, moved back to Kansas to her family while Uncle Ralph was in the military.

Dad's sister, Aunt Katherine and husband, Uncle George Irwin and children JoAnn, Dick and Glenda, lived on an irrigated farm north of Lamar. We did not see them very often because of the rough dirt roads where we lived.

In the summer of 1942 Dad went to Lamar and purchased a 1929 two door sedan Model A. WOW, a roof over our head and windows. That was living.

That Fall, I was six and a half and it was time to send me to school. What a change in my life. That meant seeing other children five days out of seven. The school was Hopewell, the same school Mom had taught at several years before I was born. It was located in Bent County west of where we lived. Bent County was actually the county that the homesteads of Granddad, Uncle Wes and Dad were located with the east end of each parcel of land joining Prowers County. Hopewell School was a one room school located two miles into Bent County. There were ten students and our teacher.

The students were Dean, Ila Jo, Gordon and Ina Bell Scranton; Hazel, Earl and Dorothy Babb; Bonnie and Jack Miller and myself. Our teacher, Mrs. Myrtle Lash, was an Aunt to the Miller children. She lived farther west on Mud Creek and only went home on weekends. She lived in a bunk house during the week at the Babb place, one half mile south of the school. The Scrantons lived where my Granddad had homesteaded, three miles southeast of the school. The Millers lived several miles west and north of the school. Bonnie and Jack rode a horse quite often to school. We were still living on the Ward place about six miles from the school.

I sat at a double desk shared with Bonnie. Jack and Dorothy were in my grade. Hazel and Dean were eighth graders. All the other students were in grades between. When my parents dropped me off to school the first day some of the other children were outside playing softball. Gordon said "Keith, you're up, get over here and bat".

We all played together at recess. Mrs. Lash played with us. Some of the games were softball, dare base and stink pot. We each had a ring (circle made of iron) that came off of a wagon wheel. Some rings were ten inches in diameter and the others were six inches in diameter. They varied from one half inch to an inch and a half in width. We had a lath (piece of wood) with a can lid nailed on the end. The lids were bent in a u shape. You would start your ring rolling and take the stick with the bent lid and push it along, running as you went. The ring fit into the bent lid. This was great exercise pushing the ring in front as you went running down the dirt trail or road. Our teacher would run along with us. On stormy days, Mrs. Lash would read or we would play some inside games. She would usually have a book that was interesting to all of us. She would read a chapter following our lunch time.

Lunch time meant we all had some kind of container that would hold our lunch. Some of us had paper sacks, but mostly it was a lard can with a lid. No one had a thermos or lunch pail like we use today. There was a cistern that some of the dads would fill part way with water.

The water for drinking at school was pulled out of the cistern with a bucket with a rope on the bail. You could flip it and make the bucket go into the water to fill it most of the way. The bucket was carried into the school near the entrance door. A dipper (a long handled metal cup) was at the bucket. We all drank from the same cup. There was no electricity and the school was heated with a pot bellied coal/wood stove.

Most families had a windmill to supply their own water for house use and livestock. A cistern was close to each house to dip water from for household use.

World War II was still on and the country needed iron for building guns, planes and other items that used metal. Scrap iron drives were going on all over America. Dean Scranton, the oldest student in the school brought his Dad's old Ford pickup to school one day. The whole school followed Mrs. Lash's car and drove all over the dryland homestead sites that had been abandoned and gathered up scrap iron (mostly old stoves, beds, wagon parts and anything else that was metal. The scrap iron was taken to Lamar and donated for the war use.

Dad and Uncle Cliff started building a pond the summer of 1943. It was located between Hopewell School and Granddad's original homestead, where the Scranton's now lived. The land was north of Granddad's old homestead which was actually what was called an additional homestead. Granddad had applied for it after he had completed the requirements of the first homestead. No one else had applied to homestead this parcel of land. One exception to an additional homestead was no mineral rights went with this land. There was Granddad's homestead, then adjoining it to the north was uncle Wes, and north of this was the additional homestead. Uncle Cliff had purchased it later from Granddad. Uncle Cliff moved a two room house on it. The draw below his house was deep and would run water from rains.

Uncle Cliff and Dad built a dam across this draw to hold back the water. They were using a John Deere D pulling a fresno behind. The fresno would scoop up dirt. You could raise up a handle on the back side and flip it over to dump dirt. This was a slow process but after many hours, with one of the men walking behind to control the long handle, dirt was scooped and dumped until a dam about two hundred feet wide was in place in the draw. There was a spillway on the far end to let surplus water pass on down the creek.

After the dam was full, they transferred catfish into the water. I remember most all of the family being there after its completion enjoying fishing and swimming. It was about seven feet deep and two hundred feet wide and about two hundred yards long. The pond is still there and it is a valuable resource for water for cattle. It is still referred to as the Clark Pond. Dad would pick me up after school and I watched it being built.

The fall of 1943 I was a second grader at Hopewell school. We would stop at Scranton's on the way and either pick them up or ride on to school with them. When the school day was over one of our mother's would pick us up. Some days we walked as far as the Scranton home, which was three miles. I would wait at their house until Dad or Mom came after me.

October of 1943 was a big change for me. Dad rented some corn pasture two miles north of Carlton, Colorado. It was in the Goodale community. This meant we had to move all our cattle. Dad and Uncle Cliff were running cows together. We drove the cattle from twenty three miles southwest of Lamar to thirteen miles northeast of Lamar. I had a welsh pony. It had first belonged to Aunt Marjorie, Dad's youngest sister and was then passed on to Jinx, Uncle Fred's daughter and then it became mine. His name was Chigger and he was a very gentle pony. He was also great to use on moving cattle. If a cow strayed from the herd Chigger would immediately turn and bring the cow back with the others. I helped move the cattle from Cat Creek to Goodale. It took two full days. The first day we made it to the Neuhold Ranch on Clay Creek east of Lamar. The second day we arrived to our destination at the Goodale land. We crossed the Arkansas River on the Morse Bridge. It was a long bridge with iron sides and top.

We moved into a two room rock house on the Carlton Corner on Road 19. Some of the changes for me to get used to was that we had trees, seven big cottonwoods. There was also electricity in the house. The electricity consisted of a drop cord from the ceiling with a light bulb hanging on the end of it. We did not have any electric appliances to use if there had been a plug in. It was great to pull a string and have light instead of lighting a wick on a coal oil lamp.

The Goodale School was one mile north and one mile west of the rock house we were staying in while the cows were on the winter corn pasture. Mom took me back and forth to school. There were more students in this school than in Hopewell school. The teacher was Nellie Brase. She had me sit at a desk. She then asked me what my first name was. I was a little shy I guess, so I told her my first name was Steven but I was called Keith. She did not hear me say I was called Keith. I was therefore introduced to all the students as Steven. I was called Steven the rest of second grade. One of the older students, Jimmy Smith became a very good friend of mine. He always called me Steve even after he knew I was normally called Keith.

He was a lifelong friend. We became neighbors in the Goodale community a few years after I was married and bought a small farm and home close to him. His family and my family had many fun times together.

When Christmas time arrived in 1943, Mrs. Brase said she needed a dad to get into the attic and get the Christmas decorations down through the small opening in the ceiling. I volunteered my dad for the job. Dad took me to school the next morning and went in with me to meet my teacher and do the job I volunteered him for. Mrs. Brase looked at Dad and said "why Dwight, I did not realize you were Steven's Dad!" You see, Dad and Mrs. Brase were classmates at Lamar Union High School graduating together in the class of 1918.

The playground at Goodale School had a big swing set with three large swings. It also had a Merry Go Round and a very large slide that had two big curves as you came down it. I used to take the wax paper that Mom wrapped my sandwiches in and sit on it. You could really get speed up as you came down the slide!

I used to ride Chigger to school part of the time. I did not use a saddle. I just had a bridle and rode him bareback. I was only seven, going on eight, but once again, Chigger was a very gentle pony. One morning as I started to school riding him it was misting. Chigger only went a few hundred yards from home and would go no further. I turned around and went back home.

Dad took me to school that day. It stayed stormy and Chigger got sick and died a few days later. Chigger was in his mid twenties when he died.

When April 1944 arrived, we moved the cattle back to cat creek driving them on horseback once again. It took two days to move them. The cattle stayed on Cat Creek until fall when we moved them north of Lamar to the Queen Lakes.

Mrs. Brase told my folks that there wasn't any use to enroll me in another school, she would advance me to the third grade and be ready for school in the fall.

Dad had purchased a half section of land from my Aunt Dorothy Clarks' dad. It was his homestead where he raised two daughters and a son. He later moved back to Kansas.

The land was located north of Lamar in Kiowa County. The Queen Lakes were in the north and east part of the land. This was quite different than the cat creek area. We had lots of trees, water and a neighbor one mile away plus lots of families within five miles, close to the May Valley community. We always had lots of people come and visit. There was plentiful fishing and lots of pheasants and cottontails, along with jack rabbits, ducks, geese and coyotes.

When we moved the household furniture to the lake house, we loaded everything on the wagon drawn by Prince and Barney. The wagon did not have rubber tires. It was original with the wooden spoke wheels. The roads were dirt with very little gravel on some of them. This made it a little rough riding, but we went slow. The first day we went about ten miles from Carlton Corner to Uncle George and Aunt Katherine Irwin's . I didn't mind the stop there as that meant I could have some play time with Dick, Glenda and JoAnn. The next day Dad put the harness on Prince and Barney, hooked onto the wagon and away we went headed for our new home.

We soon passed Alta Vista School just one-fourth mile west of the Irwin place. We had about twelve miles of travel ahead of us. Later that day we drove past May Valley elevator where farmers sold grain or also to purchase feed such as corn, milo,

bran flakes. These were sold by the gunny sack and used mostly for supplement for milk cows.

On up the road one-half mile was the May Valley Store. They supplied everything one needed in the way of groceries, gasoline and ice. We needed ice for our ice box refrigerator as there was no electricity where we were moving. Prince and Barney had a short rest while we were at the store. I'm sure we had a soda pop to drink before traveling on. I would take the reins from Dad and drive the team from time to time. They didn't need much attention though as they would go straight up the road. There would not be a turn until we came to the County line of Prowers and Kiowa on the May Valley road.

One mile north of the store we went past May Valley School. It was a big brick building with a full basement. I would start school there in the fall if the school board would accept an out-of-county student. Tuition would have to be paid from Kiowa County to Prowers County.

It was mid-afternoon and we went past the John Gentz farm, the last of the many homes that were located on the irrigated river farms. From there on, it was mainly grassland. Soon after we passed the short road to the Amity ditch rider's house, we came to the southeast corner of our new property, 320 acres total. The Lower Queen Lake was less than one-half mile north of the dike that held the water back. The lakes, five total, were all located in Kiowa County. The Queens were the south ones. They could all flow into ditches, releasing water to be used in the Amity and Fort Lyon canals to supplement irrigation water. There was a lake just south of the Queens called King Lake. It had been a lake that was not developed to any successful use because it was so deep that water could not be drained out if it was stored there. It would sometimes have very shallow water that seeped in but had a lot of alkali. The fish would not survive in it. Sometimes ducks and geese would land there.

Some people thought the lake had fish in it and would drive towards it to go fishing. No one ever got close because the salt grass surrounding the water was very swampy and hid the seep water coming out of the ground. Consequently the vehicles would drive into the swampy area and immediately get bogged down in the mud.

As we got to the corner of our property on this moving day, there was a gentleman standing there. He had gone towards King Lake and was stuck. It was about one-fourth mile to his car. Dad said "I can unhitch my team of horses and they will pull you out". Dad unhitched them from the wagon and we walked behind the horses. He hooked the team up to the car and told Prince and Barney to go. The car was pulled back to dry ground. The man wanted to pay Dad for getting him out of his predicament but Dad said he would not take any money. All the years we lived by the Lakes, numerous people would get too close to the water and get stuck. Dad never would accept anything for pulling them out, day or night. I do know that on several occasions when we had come home from town we would find several dollars in cash on the kitchen table. We realized that someone we had helped was still showing their generosity and thankfulness. Our house was never locked. Nobody had locks on their homes.

It was only one mile to our house. It was early evening the first part of April 1944 and WE WERE HOME!

The house on this property was about a quarter mile from the lake. The house was a half dugout. That is a house not deep enough to be called a basement but still down in the ground about four feet deep. It was quite small with cement walls and a steep pitched tin roof. There was a kitchen about twelve feet by twelve feet with a pantry at one end. The living room was about ten feet by fourteen feet. There were two bedrooms, one about eight feet by ten feet and the other about eight feet by five feet. That was enough for the three of us. It was cool in the summer and warm in the winter, that is if you kept a hot enough fire burning. We had what was called a monkey stove in the kitchen that was close to the door into the living room. A monkey stove stood about twenty inches high and three places about eight inches in diameter to cook on. After the first winter the folks bought a small kerosene stove with a three gallon tank on the back of it for the living room. They also replaced the monkey stove with a nice full sized cook stove. It was wood or coal and had an oven and a water reservoir on the far end and also had a overhang at the back extending up about twenty inches and partially hanging over the cooking area.

The surrounding area close to the house had some tamarack trees, three apricot trees, one big mulberry tree and two cottonwood trees. The apricot trees usually would have their blossoms frozen every spring. But about every four years we had apricots. Mom would preserve them.

The mulberry tree always had lots of berries. One day I talked Mom out of an old blanket. The mulberries were ripe. I shook the limbs and the berries fell off in bunches onto the blanket. I took them to the house and Mom made a mulberry pie out of the good berries. I remember it as being a very sweet pie.

Dad planted some elm trees. They watered them with waste water from the house. They grew fast and soon made abundant shade for the house.

Dad built a barn with a large chicken house in one end of it.

There were several private wells from the Arkansas River that had soft water. Several individuals hauled and sold their soft water. They had tanks mounted on trailers or an old truck that would hold about six hundred gallons of water. The cost was about two to three dollars per load. About twice a year the cistern needed to be cleaned out. When it was almost empty, someone was lowered into the cistern by a rope. Rags, bucket and a small container to dip the last remaining water into the bucket was let down. It would be dark and I thought it was creepy down in there. By this time I was the prime subject to be the one let down to clean the cistern as I was light enough for Dad to lower me down and pull me back up. The cistern was about ten feet deep. One time when I was down in the cistern, Mom wanted Dad to do something for her in the house. Dad said he would be right back. Here came the man in the truck with a load of water. He backed up to the cistern and got out of his truck to hook the hose to the tank to dump the water. I was still down in the cistern! I hollered, "don't dump the water, I'm down here".

At this time in my life, my parents told me they wanted to adopt two girls just younger than me. I remember going to town with them to visit with a lady about it, but the adoption did not happen. As I look back, it was not meant to be as later the family did grow overnight.

Mom told me about this time that I was adopted. She said my mother gave me up because she was not able to take care of me and wanted me to have a good home. That sure was true. I couldn't think of a better place to grow up.

Chapter Three

1944 was a DREAM COME TRUE. I learned quickly to swim and also fish. Friends came often to visit. We had lots of picnics here including family reunions. The only drawback I can think of is we were 30 miles away from Clay Creek store and Granddad and Grandma Clark. Uncle Cliff came up quite often to help with the cattle and branding. We also went back down south to help him out.

When we moved to the Lakes, Dad wanted to get another dog. I was anxious to have one for a companion for me as I was an only child. Dad thought we should get a dog that would be a hunting dog as well as a retriever since we had the lakes with ducks and geese and an abundance of pheasants. A retriever could swim out in the water to retrieve and also help to hunt out pheasants and rabbits and bring them to us after they were shot.

Dad knew a man in Lamar that raised and sold water retrievers. Mike Havey had a litter of pups born the spring of 1944. Mr. Havey worked at the Post Office in Lamar and Dad had worked as a substitute rural carrier out of Lamar in the 1930's so he was acquainted with him. Giles Strong had helped Dad in getting this part time work. Giles was a clerk and a rural carrier also.

Dad purchased a male Water Spaniel from Mr. Havey. We named him Mike. Mike was my companion, playing, hunting and just a great dog as almost every boy can remember growing up.

My horse Blondie with a cousin and a friend.

After Chigger died while living near Goodale School, I wanted another horse. Dad found one near Carlton. I don't remember much about this horse as I don't think I ever rode him. Dad took him along with some of the ranch horses on up to the property at the Lakes. The horse got into some loco weed and went crazy. Dad got rid of him.

Later in the year Dad bought me a rather large palomino. She was a good horse named Blondie. Because of her size I had trouble getting on her unless I could get her close to a wood fence to climb up and jump on her back. Later, as I grew, I was able to grab her mane and pull myself and jump up on her. One time I did a foolish thing with her.

I was walking out in the pasture and petting her and decided to ride her. I got on her and away we went. She was not bucking but she was a very fast runner. I had no way to slow her down without a bridle. She went running into the corral on full run. This was OK except she turned to go into the barn. The height of the entrance would almost shave her back as she entered. Luckily, I baled off just before she entered the barn! A fall was a lot better way to get off than to be scraped off!

It was a spring day in May 1944 when Dad told me he wanted to teach me to drive. I was eight years old. He wanted to plow out the ridge from the center of the rut road so the car would not drag when he drove over it. There was no county road into our place for a mile after we left Prowers County. Dad had bought a 1936 Ford Sedan in 1943. It was a nice car until a couple of windows got broken out on one side. Also pulling a stock trailer and hauling a few baby calves inside soon had it where it was just an old car, but it would still run. I tried to drive, but would let the clutch out too quick and either kill the motor or else I would go too fast and almost throw Dad in the air as he was desperately trying to hold the two handles of a one row lister that was made to be pulled behind horses. It did open up the center of the road and moved some of the center dirt to the tracks allowing the car to go on the road without getting high centered. What a way to learn to drive, but I loved it.

The folks planted a garden in 1944 next to the lake. I helped by carrying water in buckets from the lake to water the plants. It was a wet summer and the garden did well. We had tomatoes, cantaloupe and other small vegetables. One thing I remember that really did well was sweet potatoes. They were planted where there was a blow pile of dirt from the 1930's. I guess the ground was sandy and loose for a root crop. No one ever bothered our garden and it was close to where people had picnics and swam. It was a ways from our house.

Fall was coming and it was time to enroll in school. The problem was, we lived in Kiowa County. The school I was to go to was eight miles from home on the southeast side of Ne Noshe Lake. The school district of Kiowa County decided it would make more sense to send me to May Valley School in Prowers County. Kiowa County paid my tuition to attend Prowers County schools throughout the rest of my school years.

This was quite different than what the school in Kiowa County would have been, mainly because of the sparse population of ranch land.

May Valley School had two rooms, first thru fourth grade

and fifth thru eighth grade. There were between fifty and sixty children attending this school. Most of the irrigated farmers had hired men with families. The economy was improving as the drought was over and more jobs were available.

My third grade teacher, Miss Edith Moss was a good teacher. The teacher for the upper grades was Mrs. Nellie Guy. Mrs. Guy and Miss Moss both lived in Lamar, about eight miles south of the school. They rode to school together and also brought another teacher that taught at Clover Meadow School and dropped her off. This school was located less than four miles from May Valley School. It also was a two room school with about sixty students attending. Mrs. Laura Butler was the teacher there for the upper grades and Miss Bell was the teacher for the lower grades.

My third grade class at May Valley at that time had six students. There were four girls and one other boy besides me. Earl Gentz was in my class and one of our closer neighbors. We became very close friends. I spent lots of nights with him as well as he did with me any time our parents would allow us to do so. Earl had a sister, Louise, three years younger than me; a brother, Jack, five years younger and a sister, Virginia, who was born the year we were third graders. Virginia was born at home and I remember seeing her the day she was born when we arrived at the Gentz home after school.

When school dismissed in the afternoons, all the children went four different ways. Sometimes if no parent was there to pick us up we walked. I would always stop at Gentz's as it was only two miles north of the school. It was four more miles on to our place. I would wait there until my folks came after me. If the DeWitt's or Thompson's were at the school to pick up their children, we would all pile in one car. Sometimes there would not be room inside for all of us. The solution? Open the trunk lid or sit on the front fenders until we were all on the car.

We had Halloween programs that all the children participated in. After the program there was a box supper. All the women and the girls each fixed a box that was decorated. The men bid on the boxes the women brought and the boys bid on the boxes the girls brought. This money was used to purchase candy at Christmas to be given out at the Christmas Program. Once again this was presented by all the students. We learned special songs, mostly religious ones at Christmas.

Mrs. Guy was also a music teacher. She gave piano lessons as well as accordion lessons to me when I was a sixth grader. She taught the fifth thru eighth graders to play the flute. This gave everyone the opportunity to learn to read music and some students went on in later years to learn other instruments if they so desired.

At this time in 1944, there was no lunch program in our school so everyone carried lunches.

It was during this break in school that Dwight Heath, Ralph Turpin and Jack Buxton came to talk to Mother. It so happened that a Miss Bell, who taught first thru fourth grades at Clover Meadow had resigned her teaching position. The school board men from Clover Meadow knew that Mother was a teacher and they needed a teacher in a hurry! She agreed to take it.

What were they to do with me? Mother would arrive at Clover Meadow before May Valley was open. I did not want to leave May Valley in the middle of the school year. The solution?

I rode to Clover Meadow with Mom then rode on to May Valley with the teachers from there after they dropped off Mrs. Butler at Clover Meadow. When the weather was nice I walked west after school with Rod Perdue and stayed at his place if Mom had not caught up with me by then. Rod was a year younger than me and lived one and one-half miles from the school. This was just half a mile past Betty Bolinger. Sometimes we all three walked together. This worked out pretty good, BUT while I was at Clover Meadow waiting for the May Valley teachers to arrive, I had the privilege of carrying out the ashes and helping Mom start the fire in the big old furnace in the basement. It burned wood to start with and then coal. When I got to May Valley, it was still earlier than the other students so I had chores to do there also.

One evening when I walked home with Rod to wait for Mom to pick me up, Mrs. Perdue came running out of the house yelling for her husband, Darrell. She said "The President's dead..the President died". It was the day FDR, President Roosevelt died.

After school was dismissed for the summer in 1945, things continued about normal. Dad could not buy a tractor and I could not buy a bicycle. The war was still on and anything made of iron was not available except for the benefit of the war. The United States only produced a few 1942 models of cars and trucks. The next three years the government had all the factories producing military jeeps, trucks and airplanes. Even the cars produced were for military use only.

We still had Prince and Barney, the work horses. Dad hired his brother-in-law, George Irwin to bring his F-30 Farmall tractor to disc and plant our row crop. We had one hundred and fifty acres of dry land to grow grain. We used the grain for chicken feed and bundle feed for the cattle. This was our income, raising chickens and selling the eggs in Lamar and also selling calves. Mom's teaching income was a lot of help. She was able to buy a propane gas cook stove. This helped so much to be able to cook without heating up the whole house with the wood stove.

They had purchased a Maytag washing machine just before we moved from the south country on Cat Creek. It was equipped with a one cylinder gas engine that supplied the power to run the washer. With only the cistern and no running water, it meant we had to bucket water into the double boiler in the house, heat it up and then dip it into the washer. It sounds like a lot of work, but it sure did beat the old scrub washboard where you rubbed the clothes with your hands back and forth until they were clean. Then it was wringing them out by hand before hanging up the clothes on the clothes line.

When August 1945 came around, the war was ended after the atomic bombs were dropped on Japan and they surrendered. I remember that summer day very well. I was staying at Clay Creek store with Granddad and Grandma. People would come driving in honking their horns. They would exit their cars and yell and cheer. Everyone was so happy. Almost everybody had a close family member in the service.

Up until this time and for a while after the war there was rationing. This meant each family was issued a book of stamps. The stamps allowed you to be able to purchase things like sugar, coffee, shoes, car tires, gasoline and anything that was made out of metal, rubber, etc. I did not know what bubble gum was until after the war. The bigger the families, the more ration books they could receive.

The war was over and it was time for school to start. Dad and Mom decided it would be best if I went to Clover Meadow School starting the fourth grade. The drawback --- my Mother would be my teacher. She was afraid I might be referred to as the 'teacher's pet'. No way, she made me walk a straight line so that would not happen. Also, there was no possible way for me to avoid any homework if any was assigned. I managed to get thru fourth grade with no apparent trouble. The school was really run the same as May Valley, just different students. I knew most of the students. Once again there seemed to be only one other boy in my grade. Jim Buxton was my age and we became best buddies. We begged our parents to let us spend the night with each other quite often.

The summer of 1946 rolled around with everything remaining the same as always at the lakes where we lived. Dad was still not able to buy a used or new tractor. I could not find a bicycle. Dad hired the crops planted once again. Prince and Barney pulled the knife sled to cultivate the weeds. Dad hired the bundle feed to be cut into bundles. I would help him and we would shock the feed. This was done by placing two or three bundles together in the shape of a tee pee then we would surround these with about fifteen more bundles. That made a shock, which allowed it to dry out and also to bunch it closer to load it on a wagon to be hauled to the corral for winter feed.

Uncle George was hired once again to bring his Allis Chalmers combine and cut the milo for grain. The grain was stored in a small building that would hold several hundred bushel and adjoined the barn on one end. Any surplus grain not needed for the chickens was sold at the elevator at May Valley whenever a little extra cash was needed.

By this time I had learned to swim quite well, just learning on my own. It felt good if we had been out in the field and had grain dust on us. There was no such thing as a bath or shower every night. There was just a wash pan you did what you could with a wash cloth. Saturday night though, usually meant cleaning up good in the round thirty inch metal tub to be clean for Sunday School and Church.

School was on again in September 1946. Mother would teach again, but I would advance to the fifth grade with Mrs. Butler as my teacher. The fall was great weather permitting Dad and me to work after school and on Saturdays to stack the bundle feed next to the corral fence. Dad ordered a ton of coal to be delivered and dumped in a pile next to the wood pile, where he chopped wood with an axe.

The first Saturday before election in November we had driven into Lamar. It had begun to drizzle that afternoon. The folks bought their usual groceries such as flour, potatoes, sugar and canned good that we might need. It continued to drizzle all evening and when we went to bed it had not let up any. One end of the barn, chicken house combination was left open on the south. Dad put the 1936 Ford into the barn open end as it helped to protect it from snow or rain entering through a missing window.

Sunday morning we awoke to a very heavy snow and it snowed for several days until we had three feet of snow on the level. The cows were in the corral and the bundle feed was there also and that was a blessing. We located the coal pile under all that snow. The wood that Dad had to cut to help fuel the stove was harder to cut and bring into the house. This storm continued all week with more snowing and blowing. With no tractor, we were isolated. Even people with tractors could not handle snow of this depth.

We had a neighbor one mile away that lived in the Amity Ditch Rider's house. One day when the sun was shining and the wind was calm, Dad and I walked over to Walt Gunn's house. He mostly had to drag me over the snow. It was good to see someone, though. Gunn's had two daughters, Geraldine and Wanda. Wanda was two years older than me but we were happy to play together when we could. This family could not go anywhere either. Freida Gunn worked at J.C. Penney's in Lamar and Mother was still teaching, but everything was at a standstill.

The end of the first week Dad walked east around the south side of the Lower Queen Lake. The May Valley road had been bulldozed out. He caught a ride into Lamar that morning. That evening here he came walking back with a gunny sack over his shoulder. Someone had brought him back out on the May Valley road where he managed to walk home with some needed food.

Half way into the second week we heard a motor. We looked out and here came a bulldozer plowing snow. It was a Prowers County bulldozer. They were opening roads in Prowers County. Since we used the Kiowa-Prowers County line road, they knew that Kiowa County would not be able to reach us so they went out of their county to open up a road for the Gunn family and us.

The next day we got the old '36 Ford dug out of the barn and away we went. About a half mile from home we got stuck! There it sat and we walked back home. The next day Dad and

Walt dug a long time around our car. Walt had a '36 Ford Coupe with oversize tires and chains. They were able to pull our car out and go over to the May Valley road where we could travel slowly.

Two weeks had gone by. It was time to start back to school for Mom and me.

That week-end, here came Ralph Turpin and Jack Buxton in an old Ford pickup with chains. They had a plan for us to get back to school and Mom's teaching job. They loaded a bed, dresser and some chairs in the pickup and off we went to the Clover Meadow Church of God Parsonage. They were without a minister and the church was only a quarter of a mile from the school. Mother and I lived in the Parsonage during the week and would go home Friday evenings. We could go most of the way home. If it was too muddy, we would park our car at Gunn's and walk the last mile home. I was getting close to eleven years old and learned how to put chains on the car. If we needed the chains, I would put them on before we got into the deep mud. We would stop at May Valley Store and take groceries home.

We had a small kerosene heater that held two gallons of kerosene. I would carry a metal can with the kerosene while Mother would carry a few groceries. This way Dad had food during the week while we were gone. Dad always liked beans and would put brick chili in them.

While living in the parsonage, we did have electric lights. One evening Mother was writing a letter as we were waiting for bed time. She told me she had a sister in Wyoming whom she had not seen for about twenty years and had only visited her one time after they had been separated. Their Mother, Maude

Bentley Keeler had died of childbirth when her sister Edna was born. Mother said "she has seven children and one of them is your age, a boy and you ought to write him a letter".

I did not ever remember of any talk of cousins in Wyoming. I tried to write a letter. I am sure it was a short one as what does a young boy write about to someone he had never met? I asked Mother why we couldn't go meet them. She said "maybe next summer we could if we could save enough money for train tickets". I was excited that maybe we could take a trip and ride on a train.

Clover Meadow School had some ball games with May Valley School. This kind of made it different for me to be playing on the Clover Meadow team against May Valley, but most all of the students from both schools were friends and a lot of them were related to each other. We had May children and Heath children in both schools. There were children by the name of Gilbert, Vallejos, Adame, Ovedia, Mauch, Dieterle, Turpin, Buxton, DeWitt and one Indian girl by the name of Billie on the Hill in the Clover Meadow School. Some of these students had cousins in May Valley School with the same last name as mentioned earlier.

When 1947 arrived, cars, tractors and bicycles were being manufactured again and were soon to be available to purchase. Dad had a chance to buy a mid-sized Case tractor. He had his name placed on a waiting list at almost every tractor sales agency there was. In like turn, I had my name on the list for a bicycle.

The Case tractor that was available to buy came with a Ditch A and some other attachments that would only be used on irrigated farm land. That brought the price up a lot more

My parents and my dog Mike. I am on my new bike.

than just the basic tractor. Dad did not buy it because we were dryland farmers and did not need such equipment.

My name finally was in line for a bicycle at Allen and DeLoach's who sold Pontiac cars. They were also dealers for Schwinn Bicycles. We went to Lamar after I was notified by mail that I could buy one. It was almost dark when we got it. I had saved my own money for several years and had forty-one dollars. The bicycle sold for forty-two dollars. Dad pitched in with the other dollar and we brought it home.

I remember taking it in the house and sleeping on the couch in the living room so I could have it right beside me. My bedroom wasn't big enough to have the bicycle in there. I had learned to ride Marvin Hasser's bike so I was ready to ride. I woke up at daybreak and was outside in the cold riding it. I sure hated going to school that day as I wanted to ride that new Schwinn. I did talk the folks into letting me ride it to school in about a week. It was nine and a half miles of all dirt road to Clover Meadow School. I did ride it about once every two weeks but of course bikes in those days were single speed and I had to leave about one hour earlier than Mom did in her car to make it to school.

Clover Meadow School had a school bell in a bell tower about twenty feet up. At 8:00 a.m. in the morning the rope leading up to the bell tower was pulled and you could hear it ring for over a mile. May Valley School did not have a large school bell. They had a hand bell about six inches in diameter that was used at recess and noon. Both schools had a fifteen minute recess in the morning and one hour at lunch time.

One evening in the Spring of 1947 there was a slow, drizzling rain falling with a north wind blowing. It was not freezing but it was cold. Mom and I were heading home and the road became really slick. We were on the dry land road where there was no sand or gravel at all on the road. The 1936 Ford was sliding sideways part of the time. Mom was not the best at driving in mud and she became stuck. In trying to back up, the gear shift came out of the shifting slot in the transmission, which it would do if you moved it from reverse to first gear. Mom could not make it do anything. It was not in any gear. She said "I guess we'll have to walk". We were probably three miles from home. After about three hundred yards Mom said "I can't do it". We turned around and made it back to the car. I had watched Dad get the gear shift back in the shifter before. I was always trying to either tear something apart or put something together by this time in my life, so I told Mom to let me see if I could make the shifter go back in the correct part of the transmission. I finally got it in the right spot. We drove on slowly and made it to within a half mile of home when we got stuck in the mud again. I knew we had to walk home this time. The dike of the lake was right north of the road so it gave us some protection from the cold wind. About halfway of the walk on home, Mom started falling and saying "I can't do it, I can't get up". I would lift on her and begged her to keep trying and keep going. I was really scared, but she could see we were going to make it and she kept trying. We were both so happy to make it to that dug out home!

It was a summer day in August 1947 when Mom and I boarded the train in Lamar for Wyoming. The train was a steam locomotive. The cars were crowded with passengers. We left early that morning traveling to Pueblo and on to Denver. Mother had fixed a lunch for us to eat on the train. There was a layover at Denver for several hours. The train station in Denver was large with lots a people standing around waiting for the correct train to go their direction. Mother gave a gentleman some money to carry our suitcase and make sure we were on the right train. It was almost dark when the train left Denver. We traveled through southern Wyoming and on into Idaho, arriving in Pocatello, Idaho early the next morning. Mother rented pillows for us to have a more comfortable ride. There were not any trains that went into the part of Wyoming where my Aunt Edna and all my cousins lived. They lived in a mountain valley called Star Valley. It was near Jackson Hole and less than a mile from the Idaho border. We had to wait about six hours at a small bus station for the ride to Afton, Wyoming. The bus was just a station wagon that held about eight passengers. We arrived in Afton after about a two hour ride from Pocatello.

Aunt Edna and her oldest daughter, Goldie, along with her boyfriend DeVerle Murphy met us. DeVerle owned a car and took us to Thayne, Wyoming where the family lived. Roy Gaydon, Aunt Edna's husband, worked for large sheep ranches and lived in a sheepherder's trailer watching over the sheep. The sheep had to be corralled every night to protect them from wolves and coyotes. They were in rough mountains covered with sage brush and the sheep had to be watched in the daytime to keep them from straying from the campsite. He was not able to go home very often.

When we arrived at the Gaydon house, five of their seven children were home. They were Emmett, Rayma, Ted, Ruth and Mary Lou. I was introduced to each one. I had always been known to never know a stranger and never to be without words. However, my first comment to my cousins was "I would say something, but I don't know what to say". Emmett and Rayma were older than me and Ted was my age. Ruth was two years younger and Mary Lou was five years younger.

Most of the Gaydon children had nicknames. Gilbert was the oldest and was called Bert. Bernice Ellen, named after Mother was always called Goldie. Emmett was called Mickey, Rayma was called Bugsy once in a while. Ted always went by

Ted. His official name was William Edgar. Ruth and Mary Lou were called their given names.

The day after our arrival, Ted and a couple of his friends took me on a hike. The Gaydon house sat on the edge of a mountain. We hiked back into the mountain valley for a short distance. We came to a small canal that had mountain runoff water in it. It was probably about three to four feet deep and seven or eight feet wide. They asked me if I wanted to go swimming. Since I was a Colorado kid and swam in the lakes all the time, I guess I thought this would be a good time to demonstrate my swimming skills. We all stripped to our underwear. I wanted to be first one in the water to prove my swimming ability and show off a little. Little did I know that water in southeast Colorado is stored in lakes and water that was melted snow runoff had a temperature difference that was drastic. I guarantee you I jumped out about as fast as I had jumped in!

Mom and I spent a week in Thayne. It was a small town with people in the country living close to one another. The farmers milked cows and sold the cream to a cheese factory nearby. It was a Mormon community in a valley about ten miles wide and fifty miles long. It was a beautiful valley. Emmett wanted to come home with us. He was fifteen years old and did not go on to high school. They could not contact his Dad for permission so he stayed back in Thayne while Mom and I traveled by bus to Rock Springs. It was a good days trip. Arthur Keeler, Mother's cousin met us at the bus station. He took us to their place in Farson, Wyoming, fifty miles north of Rock Springs. That is where Aunt Edna was raised by the Keelers. She had been raised with Arthur even though he was much older than her. We planned to stay three or four days at the Keeler Homestead with the family when they received a telephone call that Roy Gaydon had come home for a few days. He said it would be o.k. for Emmett to go to Colorado and live with us for a while. Arthur and his wife Ida said they would take us back over to Star Valley to pick up Emmett. He had a five passenger 1941 Chevrolet Coupe. It was quite a trip. We went the north route up next to Jackson Hole and went over the Teton Pass road which was at that time very steep with lots of curves and quite long.

When we arrived in Thayne, I met Roy Gaydon. He was about twenty years older than Aunt Edna. I could tell he was a hard working man who made his living for his family working outdoors.

We returned to Farson and the next day Arthur took us to Rock Springs where we spent the night with Bob and Charlotte Eaton, Arthur and Ida's daughter. That evening there was a rodeo in Rock Springs. Bob took Emmett and me with him to the rodeo. The next morning we boarded the train and came home.

Dad had a retina detachment that summer in the good eye that he still had sight in. He needed surgery to regain his sight. Emmett would be a great help to care for the cattle and other chores.

Mother decided not to return to teaching when fall of 1947 arrived. Dad was the same as blind because of his childhood injury and now the retina detachment.

I returned to May Valley School as I entered the sixth grade. I was glad to return and once again join my friends there. Dad's eye surgery in Denver was not successful. The Doctors there arranged for Dad to see a world famous eye surgeon, Dr. Pischall, in San Francisco, California. This was November, so what would they do with me? The decision was made to have me go live with Grandma and Granddad Clark at Clay Creek Store. There was a small school Called Sunny Slope half a mile up the road from the store and just north of the creek.

I guess every kid that has ever had it easy at school should have followed my tracks at this school. The one room school had one teacher, Mrs. Wright. She lived in Lamar, fourteen miles north. She did not drive a car to school. She rode the Trailways Bus to school arriving at about 9:15 a.m. and the return bus picked her up at 3:15 p.m. We did not take a recess in the morning or afternoon but we had a very long noon hour, usually one and a half hours. There were two other children in school, brothers George and Gary Penley. George was just older than me and Gary was about five years younger than me. George had a nickname, Punky.

The Penley boys grandfather, George Blizzard, lived about one and a half miles east of the Clay Creek Store. He owned quite a large ranch and owned a big herd of cattle. There was a house just north of his headquarters where his daughter, Lois, and her two sons lived.

Mr. Blizzard went to the Clay Creek Store nearly every day to get or send mail. Mr. Blizzard always bought cigars when he was at the store.

There was a star route from the Lamar Post Office to Springfield that dropped off mail at the store for several ranch families who lived in the area. Granddad and Grandma never received any benefits from handling the mail, but they should have. Mr. Wheeler ran the route from Lamar to Springfield and would pick up any mail going out on his return trip to Lamar in the evening. He would also let passengers ride in his truck that needed a ride to or from the fifty miles to Springfield and back from Lamar.

I would go home occasionally on Friday afternoons after school and stay with Punky and Gary for the night and spend all day Saturday with them. We would go with Mr. Blizzard and feed cattle. There was a lot of snow this winter. He would pull a sled with his team of work horses and we would feed the cattle oil cake (protein mixed with alfalfa made into cubes about three inches long and one half inch thick). The cattle would eat the cake and graze on dry grass where they could get to it above the snow.

When we played outside at school we did whatever we three boys wanted to do. We rolled up big snow balls and stacked them in an oval shape. We managed to make an igloo with room enough for all three of us to get inside.

Highway 287 was just in front of the school. It was under construction at this time, replacing the old pavement with newer, smoother materials. The construction firm parked their bulldozers and road graders at the school area. The workmen would talk to us and let us ride on the dozer and road graders with them.

Punky and Gary had a donkey that they rode to school part of the time. One day all three of us were on the donkey and rode him some distance up the borrow pit next to the highway. We were headed south back to school when a big truck also heading south came along beside us. The trucker honked his loud air horn. The donkey unloaded all three of us in the borrow ditch in a hurry! I'll bet that trucker hee- hawed all the way to Springfield!

Mom stayed with her uncle Scott Bentley while in San Francisco. Dad was in the hospital there for over two months flat on his back after the eye surgery. Uncle Scott was a clerk in the U.S. Post Office and was able to get Mom a job at the post office during the Christmas season. I'm sure this was a financial boost to Mom as Dad had mortgaged his homestead to help with the medical expenses.

Uncle Scott was one of Mom's older uncles who did not homestead in Colorado or Oklahoma. He had left Arkansas and moved to the San Francisco area.

I spent Christmas with Granddad and Grandma Clark. I did get to go home with Uncle Cliff some week-ends as he lived about twelve miles west of Clay Creek on Granddad's homestead land. It was always a time of fun as Uncle Cliff had always been the one uncle that had lived close to us until we moved up to the lakes. Uncle Cliff and Dad still ran cattle together part of the time and always helped each other when needed.

Uncle Ralph would also take me home with him some week-ends where I could be with his three children. Floy was a year younger and Glen was three years younger. Sue was five years younger. Nancy was born a year later. Uncle Ralph was a Standard Oil agent in Lamar. He delivered gas and oil to Standards stations, such as Granddad owned and operated at the store. He also delivered bulk gas to most of the ranchers in the Clay Creek area. He would take me with him on a week-end and return me back to the store before Monday.

Emmett was at the lake house all of this time to look after the cattle there. Uncle Cliff would go up periodically and check on things.

Mother had a first cousin and her family who moved from the Oklahoma and Texas Panhandle area to southeastern Colorado. Gladys and Marshall Crabtree bought a place two miles north and six miles east of us, close to Sand Creek. Gladys mother and Mom's mother were sisters. Gladys mother, Jeanne Bentley had married Roy Brown and homesteaded close to Boise City, Oklahoma. Gladys had married a Twombly and had a son, Jim, born in 1932. Mr. Twombly died when Jim was quite young. She later married Marshall Crabtree and had a son, Robert and a daughter, Jeanne. When they moved to Colorado in the summer of 1947 they had a 1937 Ford pickup. The whole family would travel in the pickup. They had a homemade wooden box on the bed where the boys would ride. They would often stop by our place to check on Emmett and make sure he had food and was doing all right while my folks were in California.

The Walter Gunn family moved into Lamar. Mr. Gunn was the ditch rider and also the dragline operator for the Amity Ditch Company. He continued to be the dragline operator but a new person was hired to take care of the canal that ran water to fill and drain the lakes. This water was used to fill the main canal that provided water to thirty four thousand acres of irrigated land from Lamar to the Kansas border.

Herb Bellomy was hired and became our neighbor to the east. He and his wife, Ethel, had two small sons. Herb and Emmett became good friends. Herb would let Emmett help him with ditch work if extra help was needed. Emmett received an hourly wage for this.

Chapter Four

Mom and Dad returned to Colorado by the end of January from California. We were all once again at the lake dug out house. This meant I would once again attend May Valley School.

The first day back at school Mrs. Guy welcomed me with open arms. I remember her telling a student that was new to the school to move to another seat because I should have my old seat back. I was a little embarrassed over this.

1948 was both a good and a sad year. It was a great year for grass and crops. Dad was able to buy a used Allis Chalmers Tractor Model C, quite small but it had a two row mount on lister used to make rows and plant the seed at the same time.

Prince and Barney, the two work horses were getting old. The tractor relieved them from pulling our horse drawn equipment such as the cultivator, harrow and knife sled.

Dad paid one thousand dollars for the used tractor. It was small, made for farming small acreages and we were farming one hundred and sixty acres. We were fortunate to have the tractor though. Dad would start out early in the day and I would relieve him periodically. This way we could put in twelve to fourteen hour days.

Marshall had a 15-30 McCormick Deering Tractor. It had lots of power but could easily burn forty gallons of gas a day. Our Allis only used ten gallons of gas a day. We did trade some tractor work using his to pull a long one-way going over a large amount of land while he could use the little Allis to pull a harrow or small piece of farm machinery. The Allis would run ten to twelve miles an hour and only took less than an hour to go to the Crabtree farm. Marshall's tractor ran about four miles an hour in third (high) gear, so it took a good two hours to road it to our place. When I drove the 15-30 at eleven years old, I had to scoot way down from the seat to push the clutch in and use my other foot to kick it in gear. It was quite roomy after it was going. It had iron fenders and a big iron steering wheel. It was loud as it did not have a muffler, only a three inch straight pipe that would belch fire when it was dark out. There was no starter and no lights, but quite a workhorse with big wheels filled with cement for traction.

In February 1948 Gladys was ready to give birth. She went to Lamar to stay with Uncle Ray and Aunt Ella because of the long distance from their place to Lamar. It was well below zero when Patt was born. Uncle Ray thought he was not going to get his '38 Chevrolet to start to take Gladys to the hospital, but he got her there in time.

When Jeanne was born in Oklahoma, Marshall was planting corn and Gladys was in the pickup waiting for him to take her to the hospital. Marshall thought he could make one more round, but Jeanne was born in the pickup before they could get to the hospital! Marshall was a great guy, so good to his family. He was very easy going and always helping others when he could.

By now I had buddies in all parts of Prowers County since I had attended four different grade schools. I refer to May Valley School as my main rural school since I attended more years there than any others. I was really close friends with Earl Gentz as he was the only other boy in my grade. There were four girls in the same grade with us, Barbara Branom, Dorothy May, Jo Ann Thompson and Barbara Jean McBee (called Bobbie). Sometimes there were others there for a short time if their parents were part time employees of different farmers.

Kenny McBee was one grade ahead and Rod Perdue and Jimmy DeWitt was one grade behind.

I joined a 4-H Club with other area children and had a steer to fatten and show. I was training it to lead.

Dad's eyesight was not improving. We went with him to Denver to the eye doctor again. They said he should return to San Francisco to see the surgeon there again. Dad did not want to go until the fall. Uncle Fred had driven us to Denver and back. My steer had been let out with the rest of the cattle while we were in Denver. I thought he would be beside the barn wanting his extra grain I was feeding him, but he was not there. When daylight came the next day he was still not there. Dad and I took the car and drove out where the other cattle were. When he was not with them, we thought something was wrong. We drove the pasture and spotted him laying on his side. Dad got out of the car to take a closer look at him. There was a visible circle of holes in his side made from a close range with a shot gun. There was also a rifle bullet hole in him. Why did someone kill my steer? We never did know. Lots of people would hunt jack rabbits to use for fish bait. Was this an accident or otherwise?

It was close to the middle of June. 4-H Camp that year was at Camp Stonewall, west of Trinidad, Colorado. Camp was for one week and I got to attend it. It was lots of fun, with games, mountain hikes and lots of entertainment. I was 12 years old and this was my first trip away from home. Three school buses from the Lamar area took the group to camp. It took all day to get there. It was a long, slow ride and even hot, but that didn't bother young kids. There were boys and girls about my age or older. I rode on the school bus from Hartman. I soon became acquainted with another farm boy from the Hartman-Bristol area by the name of James 'Bub' McGee. Bub and I have remained good friends from that day on. To this day as I write this, Bub, his wife, Myrna and my wife, Louise remain close friends.

On the return trip from 4-H Camp my folks met me on the north side of the Court House, just south of the Elks Club building. Mom had sad news. Uncle Ray had an operation and had bled to death while I was at camp. He was like a Granddad to me. After his funeral I stayed the night frequently with Aunt Ella. I had my bicycle with me one time and I rode it uptown the next day. Uncle Cliff was in town and he said "let's go to the Pioneer Drug Store for a root beer'. Uncle Cliff was always so good to me as I was always with Dad when they worked together on the cattle drives and building fences and whatever. Well, Uncle Cliff and I had a root beer and I went back to Aunt Ella's house.

One time earlier that year Uncle Cliff's wife, Aunt Betty saw me in town. She marched me right down to the barber shop. You see, JoAnn Irwin and I had been staying with Granddad at the Store while Grandma went to Denver to visit Aunt Audrey and her family. JoAnn thought this 12 year old cousin could use a haircut. I guess Aunt Betty thought it needed some trimming before I went back home.

My Aunt Gussie also lived in Lamar. She was a Bentley, one of Uncle Ray's sisters. She had homesteaded close to where

Mother was raised. Uncle Frank had built her a home out there on the dryland. When she moved to Lamar a house mover cut her four room house in half and moved it to Lamar. It also had an upstairs room that was small. It had stairs going up to it that was more like a ladder as it was really narrow and steep. Aunt Gussie had married and divorced years ago. One day in early 1948 Dad saw Joe Hawkins. Dad had purchased the Clay Creek store from him in 1935. Joe told Dad that he had married Aunt Gussie. Dad and Mom both liked Joe Hawkins and were pleased he was now part of our family. He had a son Charles Hawkins and his wife Betty. They attended all our family get togethers along with their three sons.

I would sometimes stay with Uncle Joe and Aunt Gussie. Uncle Joe was very kind and the type of person any boy was proud to say he was your uncle.

One week-end in July 1948 I stayed with Uncle Joe and Aunt Gussie. They took Aunt Ella and me with them to Deora where Uncle Earl and Aunt Josephine lived on Grandma Addie Bentley's homestead. It was good to take Aunt Ella out of town since it had been just a few weeks since Uncle Ray had died.

On the way back to Lamar from Deora we stopped at Granddad's store for gasoline. It was Sunday and Uncle Joe knew Granddad never closed the store. We drove in and I remember seeing my folks car, Uncle Ralph's car, Uncle George's car and my relatives from Denver vehicles all in the yard. I could not imagine why all the Clark families were there and I was off with the Bentley families that day.

I went running into the store. I was told that Uncle Cliff had a car wreck and had been killed. He had been to John Duncan's on Saturday branding cattle. He had stopped by the store that evening on his way home. About two miles from home the dust was thick in the air on the road as a vehicle had passed by. Behind all the dust was a pickup. Uncle Cliff must have saw it just in time to swerve to the right. The pickup hit the side of Uncle Cliff's car at the driver's door. Uncle Cliff had some gasoline in a can in the trunk of his 1941 Studebaker car. It caught on fire. A young neighbor was in the pasture close by tending sheep. He tried to pull Uncle Cliff out but was not successful because of the heat. Someone went to the nearest phone to call the fire department and sheriff. The closest telephone? Granddad and Grandma's store. I cannot to this day imagine the shock and grief my grandparents went through. My Grandmother always kept a diary. I do not know where it is now or who in the family got it. I do know that at one time seeing in it where Grandmother had written in it when Uncle Cliff was killed. There was just two words: Cliff Killed!

Back in the early 1930's another son, Glen, was killed in Canada. He had dived into a river while he and some other friends were swimming. He was a Geologist with an oil company. He hit a rock with his head and was killed instantly. He was in his early thirty's.

I spent a lot of time in the water at the lower Queen Lake. There was a sandy beach there which was directly east of our house. I learned to swim on my own. I would go there by myself. My instruction from the folks was 'do not go in over your head'.

Some older men from Lamar had a raft made from fifty-five gallon barrels. It took about six barrels to make a raft about five feet by ten feet. The raft was left at the shore with a rope tying it to a tree to keep the wind from taking it back to the lake. One time when water was filling the lakes the raft was tied to a tree stump, but it was in about four feet of water and was pulling downward on the raft. I was by myself and decided I should un-tie the raft and re-tie it somewhere closer to shore. I had to go underneath the raft to un-tie it. The water was over my head. I could not get the rope. I had held my breath as long as I could. I raised up real fast to get air, but did not realize the raft was right over my head. I hit the bottom of something what was really hard. I saw stars but did not blackout. Pretty soon while I was still working to free the rope I noticed red all over the water. It was a cut that was bleeding quite profusely. I guess my guardian angel was busy again.

One of the older men (older that Dad was anyhow) was Bruce Newman. He did not drive but loved to fish. He would come to the lake and fish quite often, always with someone who could drive. He had a brother, Walt. Walt was cross-eyed and had a real bad limp, like one leg was four inches shorter than the other. Walt had worked for Dad over the years when he needed extra help with the cattle. Dad would get Bruce to come and stay at our house when he had to go to Denver for eye operations that took weeks of being gone. Bruce could make sure the gates were kept shut on the fence lines and feed and water the chickens as well as feeding Mike and our cats. He also had a chance to do all the fishing he wanted to.

The fall of 1948 Dad once again went back to California to Dr. Pischell for a second operation. The retina operation from the first time was not successful. This time Dr. Pischell worked on the eye that Dad had been blind in since the explosion that took his right hand off when he was a young boy in Kansas. Dad asked him what this was going to cost. The Doctor said anywhere from $5,000 to $200. I think he charged Dad about $500. Wages at that time was about fifty cents an hour.

I applied for a social security card at age twelve. I was able to help on the canal work when the ditch rider needed some extra help, such as burning weeds in the canal. There were about ninety miles of ditches in the canal portion of the lakes alone. There were eighty-two miles in the main canal where the small head gates released water directly to the farmers. I had helped Herb Bellomy fill sacks with dirt for sand bags for a dike across the canal where water was held back until the demand for the water was needed on down the ditch. I think I worked about five hours that time. This meant a check for two and one half dollars which was a sizable amount of money for a twelve year old to earn.

Dad had used Prince and Barney to pull a horse drawn mower with a sickle bar about five feet wide to mow weeds in the Comanche Canal that was eighteen miles in length from the lakes to the Sand Creek siphon where it entered the main canal, the Amity. He received seventy-five cents an hour and was paid an additional dollar and a quarter for the team of horses, making two dollars an hour, a good wage for the time.

Herb and Ethel Bellomy let me stay with them when Dad went for his second operation in California. Mom stayed with Uncle Scott again. This time they were gone about six weeks. Walt Newman stayed at the dugout to look after the cattle. This time I was old enough to also be of help. I could start the Allis tractor and pull the wagon for feeding the bundle feed to the cattle.

Herb would drop me off at Gentz's where I would go on to school with Earl, Louise and Jack.

I left my bicycle there and Earl and I would ride our bikes to school quite often. One of our crazy ideas was to hitch a ride with our bikes behind Earl's mom's truck while she took a load of grain towards the school and beyond. The Studebaker truck had grain sides and did not have mirrors that showed objects close to the back of the truck. We decided to hold onto the back of the truck that morning as she left just ahead of us. Earl was on the left and I was on the right side, staying close enough to the center back that Mrs. Gentz could not see us. She was unaware that we were back there. Everything was going great as she was slow in gaining speed. We had gone about one-fourth of a mile and was probably up to twenty miles per hours speed. Hey, that was great, no peddling, just hanging on and going down the road. Oh yes, you see, that road was gravel. Traffic had created ruts where vehicles had been driven. The road had gravel bunched up several inches in about three places. We were guiding our bikes in the hard part of the road and avoiding the loose gravel. Further and faster down the road we went. We would soon be at school earlier than usual. When Mrs. Gentz had probably reached thirty miles per hour, it seemed like fifty miles per hour to us. We really were smart seventh grade boys. That is until Earl's front tire got caught in some loose gravel. He immediately lost control and the next thing I knew, he skidded sideways, then the bike and Earl both were scraping the road as they were coming to an abrupt halt with dirt and gravel flying all directions.

I had let my grip loose as soon as Earl wrecked and was able to stop. After seeing that all he received from the wreck was scrapes and bruises, we rode on to school. We were careful not to let Mrs. Guy know the real reason why Earl's clothes were torn or why he had some cuts and scrapes on his body. Oh yes, Mrs. Gentz went right on down the road never realizing what two dare devil boys had done.

Dad was able to have partial vision in his eye after the second operation in California. He could drive around the farm and grassland but would never be able to drive on the main traveled roads.

Dad would trade off with me driving the tractor to keep up with the farm work. I made extra money helping the Crabtree's with their farming. I drove their old 15-30 McCormick Deering tractor while Marshall operated the old Baldwin Combine. We cut his wheat and also custom cut for others. The Baldwin had its own motor on it so all I had to do was drive while Marshall did the continuous adjusting it took to keep the combine thrashing the grain. Marshall purchased another tractor, a 22-36 model McCormick. It was almost identical to the 15-30 model except it was one size bigger and more powerful. It also had a road gear which meant you could go down the road about fifteen miles per hour instead of the slow pace the 15-30 did. One did not use the road gear to pull farm attachments but made it so much faster going from one field to another when needing to relocate.

Mother wanted to go see her sister again in Wyoming. Aunt Edna had been ill and her health was not improving. I wanted to go along again as I had met the cousins the year before when we went there. Besides, they lived in the mountains not far from Jackson Hole and it was beautiful and cool there. This trip Aunt Ella went along. We took the train again to Pocatello, Idaho and the bus ride to Afton, Wyoming. Emmett picked us up for the twelve mile trip to Thayne. He had an early 30's Oldsmobile that summer. After spending several days with Aunt Edna, the adults decided to have Emmett take us out in the forest where his older brother, Gilbert, and DeVerle Murphy were working. We had to travel on a logging road in back country called LaBarge Road. It was not a maintained road. There were no houses or towns, just wilderness. We all loaded into Emmett's car, kids, Aunt Edna, Aunt Ella and Mom. Several miles into the forest the car sputtered and quit. Emmett thought he had water in the gas. After draining the carburetor bowl the car started again and we were on our way. This happened about five more times. We would all get out and push the car or let it roll downhill, start the car and go several more miles.

In mid-afternoon the adults thought we had better turn around and go back home as daylight would soon be gone. About half way out of the forest road the car quit again by a logging camp that was deserted, but the buildings were still intact. There was one building that must have been separate living quarters for about five families. They were all connected with doors where one could go from one room to another. The car quit about a hundred yards from the trail down to the buildings. When Emmett drained the bowl this time he dropped the plug when removing it. No one could find it. There was loose dirt, rocks and leaves on the trail and the plug was not visible. While everyone was looking for the plug, Ted and I went down to the old buildings to look around. We could see some articles that had been left behind and we were curious as we went from one room to another. We heard a noise behind us in one of the rooms. We stood dead still and scared in our tracks. Pretty soon we heard footsteps behind the room we were in. The door behind us just barely opened and a six shooter appeared in the doorway in someone's hand! The next instant we ran out the door and probably broke any speed records ever set by two boys of our age. When we reached the car we relayed our story to the others, still scared to death. At that moment here came Emmett walking back to the car laughing. Ted and I did not know he had his gun with him. He had purchased the gun the year before when he was staying with us and working part time for the ditch company. We also did not know he had stepped down the mountainside to the deserted logging camp we were exploring. We did find the plug for the carburetor and made it back to Aunt Edna's house. This was one scare I have never forgotten!

Once again, fall of 1948 I had a 4-H steer. This one was very gentle and ran with Dad's cattle. I could go out among the cattle and right up to him and pet him. One day he was not grazing with the other cattle close to the Upper Queen Lake, where we could not see them from the house all the time. My steer never did show up. We looked everywhere in case it had gotten sick and died. It could have been very easy for one to approach it and put a rope and halter on it. Someone probably had some good eating! In those days, people did their own butchering. My luck with 4-H calves was there, but it was BAD luck.

One of our work horses, Prince became ill. He could not get better because of his age. Dad could not stand to see him suffer.

He had our neighbor shoot him in the head with a high powered rifle and not prolong his suffering. The next morning I went out to look at Prince and he was still breathing. Dad did not have a high powered rifle so he had to use an axe to finish killing the horse. The axe was used like a big hammer, a single blade on one side and a flat iron on the other. He used the hammer part to hit him in the head. It was really hard on Dad to do this to a horse he had respected and worked with for so many years. Dad sold Barney at the sale before he had to face the same circumstance with the last of his prized work horses.

Russell Ohlson and his wife Martha lived close to the Clover Meadow school area. He was the ditch rider for the Fort Lyon Canal Company. They were good friends of Dad and Mom. They never had any children but were like parents to a niece, Rosa Lee Voss, who lived at Fort Lyon, next to Las Animas, Colorado. She was my age and I spent a lot of time with her when my parents visited the Ohlson's. They treated me royally. We always had a lot of fun together when she was there during the summer and school vacations.

The Ohlson's bought a 24 Base accordion and gave it to me. They thought I could learn to play it as Martha played the accordion as well as Thelma Drumright, who owned the May Valley Store. With the help of these two women and Mrs. Guy, who gave piano lessons, I took lessons. I'm sure Mrs. Ohlson probably paid for my lessons.

Mrs. Drumright's husband, Herb, also worked for the Fort Lyon Ditch Company operating their dragline. Their daughter, JoAnn was a year older than me. Since the Ohlsons and Drumrights were good friends to my parents that gave me the

My first accordian.

chance to become close friends to Rosa Lee and JoAnn.

When April 1949 approached, I would be thirteen. The Ohlson's told Mom that if she could take me down to their place, they would take me to a movie in Lamar. Dad did not go as he could not see that good to go to the movie. It was dark when we got to their house. We knocked on the door that went into the kitchen, which was how we always entered their house. Martha said Russell was not feeling good so just the three of us would be going to town. The living room was just off the kitchen. Russell was in there with a dim light on. Martha told me to go tell Russell good-bye and we would head on to town. Just as I entered the living room a bright light was flipped on and outburst a dozen or more kids hollering 'Happy Birthday'. All my friends from May Valley and Clover Meadow schools were there. They sure gave me a surprise. We played games and had lots of ice cream and cake. This was my first surprise birthday and one to remember, 'what fun'!

That summer, Ray and his son, Phil Gilbert started giving me orphan lambs. They ran a large herd of sheep as well as cattle. By the end of lambing season I had about eighteen lambs. This proved a lot more profitable than raising steers for someone to shoot or steal.

At the end of summer my cousin, Dick Irwin and I rode the train to Denver and stayed with Aunt Audrey and family. We were to purchase school clothes because they would be cheaper in Denver at May D & F. I had about twenty-five dollars to spend on jeans, shirts and other items of clothing. Aunt Audrey said "you boys get in the front of the line and be the first inside the store". We rode the streetcar several blocks away from their house. We found the May D & F early so we were the first in line to get into the store for this big back-to-school sale. Now I'll tell you, I had helped work cattle and sheep that had been penned up. You did not want to be just standing in front of the gate when it was opened. Little did Dick and I realize that a bunch of women could go 'wild' when the store doors were opened. We got an education real quick to move fast and stay out of the way of Denver women! We did buy our school clothes. Our cousin, Otis Angell drove us around Denver and we had fun together. Aunt Katherine came to visit Aunt Audrey and drove us home.

I was now an eighth grader. The feed in the field was bundled and the grain was cut. I would still ask the folks if I had any brothers or sisters and what my name had been. It was always the same answer, "I think your name was Callender and your birth mother was very young from northern New Mexico. She could not care for you so she gave you up at the orphanage, where we got you". That was all I needed to know, but being an only child when nearly all the other children in school had sisters or brothers made me wish I had other siblings. Oh well, I had my dog, Mike, some cats and a rabbit to play with. Also I would stay nights with Jim Twombly or Rod Perdue or Earl Gentz. Also I would stay all night or week-ends with my Irwin cousins. They also liked to come to our place as there was fishing and ice skating in the winter.

I would take baling wire and wrap around my bicycle tires to make chains so I could ride on the ice. The ice would freeze quite thick in those years. We had to keep it cut open so the cattle could drink water. It would get a foot thick so the lake was frozen over for several months.

Russell and Martha gave me a pair of hockey ice skates. I would live for the time I could ice skate in the winter just like swimming in the summer. We were still without electricity, running water and a telephone, which did not bother me because I did not know different. We had a power pack radio that was good for a month on one battery. Until we had the power pack, a six volt car battery would last about one week before taken to town to be charged again.

Dad always listened to some murder mysteries such as Intersanktum, The Squeeking Door and other programs that had me almost afraid to go to bed or outside to our pathway outhouse. The programs I did enjoy were Fiber McGee and Molly, Gildersleeve, People are Funny with Art Linkletter, Bob Hope and Red Skelton.

There were a couple of times that summer while I was still an only child at home that I can remember being frightened.

One was the time the Stickler boys, Gene and Tom, told me about catching pigeons in a house owned by Harry Gist. They said they were going to tame them and have pet pigeons. Charles McPherson lived just past Perdue's on the road to the lakes where I lived. We decided to stop at the house and see if we could catch some pigeons. Charles was an only child like me and said he would love to have a pet pigeon. We entered the house but did not have any luck capturing any birds. The house had broken windows throughout. When we came out of the house there sat Mr. Gist in his car. He said he was tired of kids breaking windows and going into the house. He told us he was going to take us to Lamar and have us put in jail. We pleaded with him that we did not break the windows and this was the first time we had been in the house. He said he did not believe us, but if we could run towards home and go as far as the bridge on the May Valley seep ditch in a minute, he would let us go. It was about five hundred yards to that bridge. We both ran as fast as we could and never looked back until we reached that bridge several minutes later. We then stopped and looked back. He was nowhere in sight. I'll bet he laughed all the time we were running towards that bridge.

The other time that year was in the summer time in 1949. Dad had made a fish trap out of hail screen. We also had a seine, a net about thirty feet wide. With a man on each end, you could pull the seine towards shore line and catch a fair amount of carp. If you had any cat fish, the law was to return them back to the lake. Dad had a seining permit issued by the State. The Hassers, McEndree's and other family groups used to come to our place and seine fish and we would have a big fish fry.

A fish trap usually caught cat fish. This was not legal according to the regulations of the State Game and Fish Division. Most of the landowners around the lake had fish traps. I think the Game and Fish Warden turned his head on the landowners and their fish trapping. Dad always let fishermen, hunters and people wanting to picnic on his land and have free access to all of the above.

We made a homemade trap that was three feet long and twenty inches in diameter with one opening at the end shaped like a funnel. We would shoot a jack rabbit, skin it and tie it in the middle of the trap. The fish would go in but could not find their way out. The trick of the trap was to place it in a least four feet of water or deeper. We would take a gallon glass jug to float on the water and tie a small rope to the trap from the jug. We would wade out in the lake with it and leave it overnight or for a twenty-four hour period.

Two brothers from Lamar who worked at the local butchering plant knew Dad and they wanted some cat fish. They knew that we had a fish trap and could provide the fish for them. I knew where the trap was located by a certain landmark and about how far from shore the trap was. Dad was gone the afternoon they came driving in. Just Mom and I were home.

The two brothers had more liqueur than they should have had. They had a couple of boys along that were just younger than me. The brothers had been driving recklessly and the two boys in the back seat were bloodied from being tossed around in the old car. When Mom told them Dad was not home, they insisted that I go along to find the trap. I got a little worried. I did not know the boys. The men drove so fast and bounced all over the rut road that I became scared. When I told them the trap was straight out in the lake from a certain spot that I had them stop, they insisted that I take my clothes off and go out in the lake and retrieve the trap.

It was about one hundred and fifty yards out in the lake. That did not bother me, but their rough talk and being really drunk scared the living daylight out of me. When we got out of the car and they kept insisting that I go out in the lake, I thought of a plan of escape. Just directly on the opposite side of the car was a field with our bundle feed. It was about one hundred feet from the car. It ran back toward the house, almost to our barn. Instead of undressing and going towards the lake, I took off on a very fast run towards the field. I entered the field and was out of sight and made my way back to the house via the thick feed. When the men left, they did not stop by the house and I was relieved, as I'm sure Mom was too when I related my story to her as soon as I came storming in the door.

The old 1936 Ford became a problem that fall so Granddad Clark had a 1929 Model A that he was not using and let Dad take it. Model A Fords were considered an old, but reliable car and simple to keep running. This was good enough for the three people in our family. The motor needed some work. Russell Ohlson came to the rescue. Russell used Model A's to ride the ditch and also had a coupe for their personal car. He knew every detail of Model A's. He took the motor out of the 1929 and rebuilt it. After the overhaul it ran like a new one. Russell would not take a dime for anything he did to it.

Mother took the bus to Salt Lake City the fall of 1949 to visit Aunt Edna, who was battling cancer. There were no treatments to fight the cancer in 1949.

Christmas was past and I was still wishing that when Mom and Dad had visited Social Services earlier in my life, we could have adopted two girls so I could have had other children to play with. Our distance between the neighbors at May Valley and Clover Meadow made it hard to have any companionship in the winter time. I had to be careful not to play too much outside in the cold weather with Mike my dog because I would get earaches that would sometimes last a week with a high fever. We would spend the evenings playing cards. Mother would also read and Dad would listen to his radio programs if the power pack battery was charged. I would usually read if I had anything to read and also listen to the radio with Dad until bed time. My life was about to have one of the biggest changes ever to happen to a thirteen year old boy.

Chapter Five

It was December 31st, New Year's Eve. We were at Russell and Martha Ohlson's when they received a telephone call from Aunt Katherine trying to locate my folks. She had received word that Aunt Edna passed away that day.

Mom and Dad took the bus to Star Valley Wyoming for the funeral. I stayed with Aunt Katherine and Uncle George while they were gone. Aunt Katherine drove me two miles west to the May Valley road to ride on to school with Mrs. Bolinger. The hot lunch program was at the school now and Mrs. Bolinger was the cook. She had moved into Lamar but drove out every day to the school. Her daughter, Betty, was a year younger than me but still attended the country school. JoAnn was in high school and Dick and Glenda attended Alta Vista School.

My love for Model A Fords grew, as it turned very cold the first part of January 1950. Uncle George had a 1946 or 1948 Chrysler with a straight six cylinder motor with only six volt electrical power. It would not turn over fast enough to start. I told Aunt Katherine I would start the Model A. She laughed at me as that old ford was over twenty years old by then. The old Model A had a feature Henry Ford put on the Model A's that you could turn the choke counter clockwise a turn that would make the gas mixture richer. This enabled the car to start easy if the battery would just crank the motor. I guess our Model A had a good battery as the ole ford just started right up even though it was well below zero degrees outside. No more laughing at me

I am ice skating with Mrs. Ohlson on the lake.

that morning, just amazement!

Uncle Fred lived in Denver and picked up the folks at the bus terminal in Denver and brought them back to Lamar when they returned from Wyoming. His trunk was full of suitcases and inside the car with him were Dad, Mom, cousins Rayma, 15; Ted, 13; Ruth, 11 and Mary Lou, almost 8 years old. Our family had grown from three to seven within ten days! I did not know that Mom and Dad would bring the four cousins home to live with us. There were two older brothers, Gilbert and Emmett and one older sister Goldie. She was married and had a small child. They were unable to care for and raise the four younger siblings. Star Valley was a Mormon community and the church had enough families in it and decided they would divide the four younger children up and raise one, but they would be separated. Dad would have no part of that. Even as hard up and with really no room in our little half dugout, Dad said we'll take them all and keep them together".

Now togetherness it was. Ruth and Mary Lou went to my little room, just big enough for one small bed. Rayma slept on the couch and Ted and I went out to the entrance going down the steps where there was just room enough to put a mattress on each side. That was all that would fit into that small space, no heat at all, just a tin roof over our heads and a wooden wall on the sides. Any barn would have been just as warm.

That lasted less than two weeks. The family decided that the old chicken brooder house would make Ted and I a much roomier and warmer place to sleep. The brooder house was about eight feet by twelve feet. Brooder houses are not used much in today's time. A brooder house was used to raise baby chicks after they were hatched from the eggs in an incubator. The incubator kept the fertile eggs at a constant temperature until time to be hatched out of the shell. Once the baby chicks were hatched they would be put under a brooder stove, which was usually a funnel shaped metal cover. This was heated with kerosene fuel with a wick much like the old kerosene lamps. This would put off heat to keep the baby chicks warm until they were big enough to be moved into a larger area where they could run around and grow. If you had electric power, a heat lamp could be used instead of the cone shaped kerosene heater. If heat was not kept at a steady level, sometimes the little chicks would pile up on one another to keep warm and suffocate the ones on the bottom of the pile. We usually raised about one hundred chicks. When they were grown, the male roosters were used for eating and the hens were kept for laying hens. We sold the eggs for money.

The room was large enough for a double bed and we also put in Mother's old kitchen coal stove. We built a fire when we were ready for bed and it would last most of the night. We slept under about six heavy blankets so were comfortable sleeping.

In the morning we dressed in a hurry and ran the seventy-five feet to the dugout when it was below freezing weather.

Kiowa County School District agreed to let our new family attend May Valley School with me. Ted, Ruth and Mary Lou started school within a few days of arriving. Rayma would wait to start high school in the fall since it was the middle of the school year.

The weather pattern had returned to a very dry spring with a lot of wind. This made it bad on us as the half dugout windows started at the ground. The dirt would sift through into the house covering beds and everything else inside with dirt, deep enough for one to write their name on it. The dirt would drift like snow drifts on the fences, barns and anything else that could catch dirt.

Rayma was always thinking of dumb things to do. One day when Ted and I got home from school she had taken a bottle of black shoe polish and decorated the brooder house. She drew all kinds of pictures on it. The brooder house was painted red so the black shoe polish showed up real sharp.

To this day, Rayma still reminds me of the black plastic pipe about ten feet long that Ted and I stuck through a knothole we pounded out of the side of the brooder house. After inserting the plastic pipe through the hole, we had our own indoor plumbing! This was a quick, easy way not to have to go outside in the cold. Rayma saw the pipe coming out of the brooder house. When she picked it up and yellow liquid that was trapped in part of it ran out, she knew just what it was used for!

One evening when the weather was warm, Rayma and I walked down to the lake. When we got there, we decided to go on around the dam and visit the ditch rider. By the time we got to their house the sun had completely set and it was almost pitch dark. Their coal oil lamp was on in the living room and we could hear them talking. One of the dumb things we did was to walk up to the window and scratch on the screen with a stick. The screen did make a startling sound this calm evening. Of course the blood curdling scream that Rayma let out sounded like a cougar or some wild animal. The light in the house immediately went out and we could hear footsteps moving around inside the house. We decided to squat down behind a lilac bush that was about eight feet tall. We could hear the back door open onto the screened in porch. Just about the time we were going to stand up and say something, a shotgun went off. The BB's went just above us through the top of the bush. I immediately jumped up screaming "don't shoot, don't shoot, it's me". We should have known that you don't sneak up to a house isolated in the country and pull a prank like we did. The ditch rider told us later that he could see us hiding behind the bush, but did not know what it was. He said if we had run he would have shot us! No more tricks from Rayma and I on that level of fun.

Jim Twombly was to graduate from Lamar High School May 1950. He rented a room with some other boys and lived in town during the week and went home on week-ends. The first part of May Jim thought he should take Ted and me to high school for a day to prepare us for entering high school that fall. He wanted to prepare us country cousins for the big change. After that visit we both knew we wanted to go into agriculture and FFA. I was anxious to learn more about engines, welding, etc.

Summer was fast approaching when we received word that Roy Gaydon, the father of Rayma, Ted, Ruth and Mary Lou, was seriously ill. He was with his other three children in Star Valley but it was decided that if Rayma returned to Thayne she could help care for him. He passed away while Rayma was en route. Due to the costs involved it was not possible for any of us to go to his funeral.

Dad located another half round top brooder type house in town that had been lived in and never had chickens in it. A school teacher had rented it and was leaving town so it was for sale. It was rounded from the back to the top and part way down then came straight down the front side. It had several windows and a door on the flat side and was bigger than the one Ted and I slept in. There was room for two full size beds and the stove plus a couple of chairs. Dad was able to buy it and a neighbor hauled it with his farm truck to our place. Ted and I thought we had a mansion! We unloaded it by our three apricot trees just south of the other one. This provided some shade in the summer.

Rayma called from Wyoming to say she was in love and wanted to get married. My folks gave her their blessing and did not object. She married Elmer Wolfley who was a prince of a guy and very much accepted by all of us.

That fall, Gilbert left Wyoming and along with Goldie and Deverle, came to Colorado to visit their sisters and brother. Emmett had joined the army by then. Gilbert decided to stay and live in the newer brooder house with Ted and I. He got work with the hay mills and became part of our family.

Gil had a 1939 Chevrolet which was newer and longer than the Model A the folks were driving. It helped when he could take us somewhere.

Dad bought a 1936 Chevrolet to use which also made it easier for all of us to travel to and from Lamar.

When Ted and I started high school there were no school buses out of Lamar, so parents just carpooled or some students stayed in housing in town provided by those renting out rooms. However, in the fall of 1950 the Ford dealer in Lamar purchased a new Ford bus to be used for picking up high school students. It cost ten dollars per child per month to ride. Once again, Kiowa County School District said they would pick up the tab for Ted and I to ride the bus. We had to meet it on the north end of the route, which was at Perdue's corner just east of their house. This was about four miles from our place. Gil would take us to and from town when we had nightly FFA meetings. One time our Ag Teacher had Ted and I stay the night with him and his wife after a district meeting when it was quite late getting back to Lamar. He was good to us as most of the teachers were.

We would also occasionally stay the night with Aunt Gussie and Uncle Joe, sleeping in that bedroom upstairs that was accessed by going up a ladder stairway.

We had been without electricity and a telephone all these years. In the fall of 1950 a telephone line was put in at the dugout. There were fourteen people on the same line. We would only hear one-half of the fourteen rings.

Our code was one long and two short rings. We had to go through an operator. Our telephone number was 0188 J 1-2. The J 1-2 meant one long and two shorts. All the country lines had a lot of people on the same line. I remember Uncle George and Aunt Katherine's number was 0283 R-5 meaning five rings for their number. Uncle Ralph and Aunt Dorothy lived in Lamar and their number was 61 W, only one ring. Quite a difference that was. Granddad and Grandma at Clay Creek Store still had the old telephone that you either rang the bell by turning the crank to get the operator or else if you called someone on your same line, you could crank their code yourself. Their number was 012 F 1-2, which like ours was one long and two short rings. Why do I remember all these numbers? I don't know, I just do.

When Christmas time 1950 came there was not any extra money for things that were not necessary. There were gifts from relatives that were more able to share. I know that most of Dad's brothers and sisters all sent gifts to us kids as everyone on the

Clark side accepted the Gaydons as part of their own family. Granddad and Grandma Clark had a lot of grandchildren and they included the Gaydon children as their own.

I remember very clearly Dad's best friends, Aaron and Oscar Hasser and their generosity. Aaron and Ruth came driving in just before Christmas with their car full of packages for us kids. They knew what a struggle it was on the folks to keep their heads above water. The gifts they brought were nice shirts and sweaters for Ted and I as well as some nice dresses and other clothing for the girls. Aaron had married Ruth later in life. She had been a Catholic Nun before she became a Registered Nurse. She was an angel in disguise. She died way too young of cancer. Not having any children of their own, our family as well as their nieces and nephews were all children to Aaron and Ruth.

The Gaydon children were adjusting well to the lifestyle we had on the open plains. Quite a difference from the mountain valley of Wyoming.

When school was out for the summer Ted and I both got jobs driving tractors or helping the ranchers with their cattle operation. I mostly worked for Marshall Crabtree helping one-way (plowing land with a disc that could only turn one way). I also did some work for some of the irrigated farm neighbors learning to irrigate. Ted went down south to Aaron Hasser's ranch and helped build fence and work cattle for a while.

When I was helping at Marshall's, Jim Twombly was also doing a lot of field work, which meant we would really be dirty at the end of the day. We would usually go back towards home and go swimming in the lake to clean up. Jim was also very innovative and had mounted a fifty-five gallon barrel on a stand next to the windmill. When the barrel was full of water, he would let the windmill go back to its normal route of flow into the stock tank. In the meantime, the barrel of water was out in the open sun. The sun would heat the water up considerably, as the well water is about sixty-two degrees when it comes out of the well. Jim made a shower head hooked to the bottom of the barrel. We would open the valve and take a shower. Not hot, but usually warm. I thought this was a modern convenience.

Ted and I both were home enough to help with the farming there. We still had to grow feed for the cattle and grain for the chickens. We had a four wheel trailer that would hold seventy bushel and we would pull it to the elevator with the small Allis Chalmers C tractor when we had extra grain to sell. It took nearly one hour to drive from home to the elevator at May Valley and another hour to come back home.

I was now ready for my sophomore year in high school. It was mostly the same routine except for Ag. It was now a two hour class instead of one hour like the freshman year. Freshman year the Ag boys had constructed one of the first buildings at the fairgrounds in Lamar. I was excited to get back in class as most of the time the second hour was out in the shop. I had learned the basics of welding, but was ready to actually build something and to also overhaul some engines. After Dad had purchased the 1936 Chevy, he had parked Granddad's Model A. Something had happened to the motor. My cousin, Bob DaVault gave me a motor. I took it apart and it had a broken piston. I finally found another old engine that I took the piston out of. I was fifteen years old at this time and really excited the day I used wire stretchers on a limb from a cottonwood tree to get the engine installed into the car. When I got everything hooked up, it was snowing, but I still kept working until I got the car started. I drove it over to our mailbox one mile away and back home. I knew I just could not wait until I turned sixteen and could buy my own car!

Dad bought a rebuild kit for the Allis Chalmers C tractor and let me take it to the Ag Shop to install it. I installed new sleeves, pistons and ground the valves. I also gave it a new bright orange paint job. Orange was the color of Allis Chalmers tractors. I had the supervision of Lloyd Lawson, my Ag teacher, but I did most of the work myself.

The weather was still very dry with occasional blizzards the winter of 1951-52. We still lived in the half dug-out with the boys in the small out building. There was no water in the house except the bucket by the wash stand. A five gallon bucket was used for waste water and dumped on the trees when emptied. Gilbert had gone back to Wyoming the fall of 1951 so there was just Ted and I in the building outside. The path to the outside toilet was always busy with all of us using it. We did not tarry in there very long as it was winter.

In December 1951 right after Christmas, Dad and Mom were invited to ride with Herb and Thelma Drumright to visit Russell and Martha Ohlson who had moved to Arkansas. They let Ruth and Mary Lou stay with relatives while they were gone. Ted and I stayed home to feed the cows and break the ice in the lake for the cattle to drink.

There were several things that happened during this week's time that could not have been what parents would appreciate coming home to. One such incident was the day we took the

1936 Chevrolet out to feed the cows their protein cubes. The cattle that morning were clear up to the north end of the place, between the upper and lower Queen Lakes. It had really been cold, the ice where we chopped it open for the cows was about eight to ten inches thick. That morning after caking the cows we knew the lake travel was much smoother than the dirt road. We had watched other people drive on the ice. One could go fast, hit the brakes, turn the steering wheel or whatever and it was impossible to wreck a car because all it would do was slide on the ice. It was about 9:00 a.m. in the morning, the sun was shining bright, the temperature about at the freezing point and the ice would not melt fast. We got on the ice and were traveling at a fair speed of 25 or 30 mph when I turned the wheels and hit the brakes. WOW, that was a good skid going around and around. When we stopped sliding, the motor died! Like normal, when that old chevy was very warm or a little hot the motor would sometimes fail to start. This was one of those times. We were only out in the lake about seventy five yards but the water would be about five or six feet deep under us. After failing to get the car to start, we were a little concerned. The heat from the motor and tires were making the ice below us start to melt. I told Ted we would have to push the car to shore before it fell through the ice. We both started to push it, however, you don't push a car sitting on a lake of ice when your shoes do not have cleats in them. I was really in a panic. I did not think we would have time to run home to get the tractor, and it might not be able to have enough traction to move the car. Ted always had a quick thinking mind when we were in trouble. He said "I think I know what we can do". I said "what is it, we need to do something in a hurry". Ted said "let me take the axe we used to chop the ice and I'll get behind the car and chop a little cup behind the wheels where we can put the heel of our shoes and push the car a few feet". It would roll about three or four yards each time. We both worked our tails off getting the car to shore, but it worked. Oh yes, as soon as we were at the edge I tried to start the car and it just started right up!

While Dad and Mom were in Arkansas, my twin cousins, Dwight and Otis Angell came to Lamar to visit relatives. They were also cousins to Bob, Mary and Virginia Strong. Dwight Clark Angell, named after my Dad, was going into the war. The Korean War was on and he was a pilot. Dwight's plane was shot down off the China coast. It was thought he was captured and taken prisoner, but he never returned after the war was over. Dwight and Otis visited Ted and I and went jack rabbit hunting with us. That was the last time I was to see Dwight.

Ted and I shot a jack rabbit and decided to make a hamburger. We dressed it out, cut off the meat and ground it up through the meat grinder. He must have been a great granddaddy. I'm sure if we had ground up an old car tire, it would have been just as tender.

School lunches were not available in high school. You either went home if you lived close by, took your lunch or else you could buy a hot dog for fifteen cents and a root beer for five cents. If you were extravagant you could get a double hot dog for twenty cents. A quarter would get you by. I usually bought a hot dog and root beer and used the other nickel for an ice cream cone or used it to play pool at the pool hall. Ten cents would pay for a pool table with a rack of balls. Two of us would each put in a nickel and play a game of pool.

Mrs. Tefertiller, grandmother of Jimmie DeWitt and Lorene James lived about three blocks from the high school. She cooked a noon meal for her grandchildren. Eleanor DeWitt and Jessie James were daughters of Mrs. Tefertiller. She said she would feed some other students from the May Valley area for a small fee. I think it was fifty to seventy-five cents each. We had food like mashed potatoes, gravy, green beans, a meat dish and a dessert. It was a well balanced noon lunch. In addition to Jimmie and Lorene, there were JoAnn Drumright, Rod Perdue, Ted and I and a girl from Hartman. This worked out great for all of us country kids. Someone turned her in to the State of Colorado for not having a café license. She had to quit feeding all of us except her two grandchildren. It was back to the drug store to eat, unless we could make it to the bar at Duckwall's.

The spring of 1952 was upon us and I was going to be getting my driver's license as April 4th I would be sixteen. Early in March I sent in to the State the necessary paperwork for a birth certificate. My first and only one had burned up when I was just under five years old. I had not replaced it as there was no real reason to.

The day I received my birth certificate, Dad and Mom opened up the mail and told me when I got home from school that they hoped I would not be too disappointed as my birthday was actually April 1st, April Fool's Day. I was three days older than I thought.

My classmates that were getting their first driver's license had a ninety day wait to obtain a full license to drive without a licensed older driver along. Since we lived in Kiowa County with Eads as the County Seat, I went there to take my driver's test. Mr. Bradbury, the County Clerk, had me drive around the block. When we got back to his office, he gave me my license with no restrictions. The next day I managed to talk my folks into letting me drive to school. My classmates could not believe that I had an actual full license to drive alone.

School was out the last of May. I had a job working for the Amity canal company operating a bulldozer pushing dirt out of the canal on the Kicking Bird ditch that ran water to the Lakes. Ted got a job with Louis Brase on his irrigated farm. Ted and I decided that if the Amity and Mr. Brase would okay it, we would trade work with each other. It was agreed. I would work one week for the Amity and the following week for the Brase's. Now I needed a car to get to work.

Granddad and Grandma Clark by now had sold the Clay Creek Store to the Lamborns'. They took a two story brick home in Lamar on trade for part of the payment. They also owned a smaller, newer home on South Ninth Street. It was quite a distance to walk to downtown. The brick home was across the street from the Library. With the encouragement of their children, they moved into the newer, smaller home.

Two houses down from their house on 9th Street was a Model A Ford that had been parked for several years. It had been running when it was parked. It was a 1930 Two Door Sedan. I agreed on the price of forty dollars. I spent the night with Uncle Ralph and Aunt Dorothy. Uncle Ralph was the Standard Oil Company dealer. He gave me five gallons of gas. I had brought in an old battery and a hand pump to air up the tires. Early the next morning my cousin Glen Clark and I aired up the tires and put in the battery. I had filed the points in the distributor and put the crank into position, as the battery was low. After a little cranking and choking, the old Ford was running and ready to drive. I went to the Court House where I bought a temporary permit and off I went!

I needed that car so Ted and I could trade off to get to work. The one that was working at Brase's would get dropped off and the other went towards Lamar to the Leland Good place. His

My first car, a 1930 Model A Ford.

son, Jack, was one of our best friends. I had known Jack since first grade because we were in the same Sunday School class at the First Baptist Church.

The Model A was left at the Good place all day and Clyde Shelton would stop there to get whichever one of us that was working for the canal company that particular week. We rode with him to the canal that was being cleaned out just west and north of Hasty. Mr. Shelton operated a Lima Dragline, a big machine on tracks, while Ted or I ran the bulldozer close by.

About the time to go back to school, Rod Perdue and I decided that girls were getting more attractive to us. We asked the Smith sisters to go on a date with us to the movies. Levina and Virginia lived about halfway from home to Lamar. We took my Model A to pick them up. Just before we arrived at their house a big thunderstorm came up. It both rained and hailed. When we arrived at the driveway to their house the water was above the running boards on their dad's car. Water was running throughout their house, which was lower than the surrounding roads. The girls were busy helping move things from the floors to the beds or tables to try to keep them from water damage. They hollered out to the road where we were parked and said they had better stay home and help their Dad and Mom. Besides, they would have had to wade in water knee deep to reach us at the roadway. Rod and I decided we had best turn around and go back home, due to the fact we would surely have some mud to plow through to make it home. The road to Rod's house was gravel but it was just a dirt road the next four miles on home. When we got to his house, it had not rained much. When I got home it had not even sprinkled. When I went walking in, Dad and Mom wondered if we had been stood up. That was how my first date turned out.

Dad's 1936 Chevrolet was always breaking down. Usually it was the transmission, broken axel or motor that was the problem. It had a tight, warm body and was comfortable to ride in the winter. Dad had a chance to buy a 1937 Chevrolet from a friend who had purchased a new Plymouth. He sold Dad the 1937 pretty cheap. We thought with both cars we could use parts from one to the other. The 1937 Chevrolet had at one time been wrecked and was put together with lots of lead in the metal. It soon began flaking off. The frame had been broken and just plate welded together. If you parked where it was not level the doors would not open or if you got them open they would not shut. We also soon learned that the 1937 model was a master model and the 1936 model was a standard model, so a lot of the parts would not interchange.

I decided I would fix up the 1936 Chevrolet and drive it instead of the Model A, since it had a good heater and a radio. This would be much nicer to haul girls in. I soon discovered it was way too expensive for me to keep in running condition so back to my old trusty Model A.

I made the Ag judging team my junior year in high school and got to go to Fort Collins with the other boys on different teams. My team was judging chickens of all things! I did all right but did not place, just average. The thing I most remember about the trip was staying in a motel that had a television. I had never seen one before. You had to put quarters into it for thirty minutes of T.V. We Ag boys all pooled our quarters and watched this black and white screen all evening. We had the option to go to a movie, but this way we could all go back home and tell people we had watched T.V. Oh Boy!

Most of my memories in this part of my life are what I learned in Ag class and FFA. I was crazy about overhauling motors and welding. I would help overhaul anything from a one cylinder engine to a V-12 Lincoln. When it came to welding, I liked to arc weld and also braise with a torch. Kids with cars liked to put noisy mufflers on them, especially the Ford V-8's as you could put dual exhausts on them. We would put Hollywood, or today they are called glass packs, on the cars. They usually had a deep mellow sound. Sometimes the police would get on to us if they were too noisy and tell us to take them off or else! If it was a stock muffler like the oval shaped ones, we could get by with a noisy one.

I would take a hacksaw and cut one end of a stock muffler off, take all the insides out, put the end back in place and weld it on. It appeared to be a stock muffler, but it did not have the quiet sound as the original. The police let us go since it was a stock unit. I did this for a lot of other students.

I obtained a radio from a junked car and mounted it in my Model A, so I thought I was right up-town. I still did some bulldozer work on the week-ends for the Amity canal. That gave me spending money for an occasional date to go to the movies or roller skating.

The summer between my junior and senior year I worked one hundred percent on the bulldozer and Ted worked for Louis Brase full time.

The ditch rider moved from the lake house that was on the south side of the lake about three-fourths of a mile from our dugout house. Bill Pattie, the Superintendent for the Amity offered the job to Dad. He knew Dad could not drive out of the local area of the two Queen Lakes, but with Mother to drive for him, Mr. Pattie was sure, as well as the Amity Board members, that Dad would make a good reservoir patrolman. Dad accepted the offer and we moved in August.

This move was a milestone in my life. Here are all the plusses: the house had three bedrooms, a kitchen, dining room, living room and a large front porch. There was also a basement to be used as a cellar and a large screened back porch. We also had a two car garage and a small barn. This land joined our land so the cattle could use the land and barns at both places and be in the same pasture. The house had a kitchen pump and a sink that drained outside. There was no electricity of course but the line was in the process of being constructed as we were moving in.

Here I was with Ted, Ruth and Mary Lou with big rooms and we would for the first time have electric lights. My senior year in high school then would not be with the old kerosene lights.

The Amity Board hired a man from Chivington, Colorado to come and wire the house for electricity. They let me help him. I think since I was just seventeen they needed me to do all the attic work. The rural electric association would not turn on any electricity at the pole until the house was wired. This meant I had to use a hand brace bit to make all the holes in the plates in the attic. It took one week to do the wiring. My knees were so sore from crawling around on the rafters all week, that my foot slipped and I went thru the ceiling in the kitchen but caught myself with my arms before falling eleven feet to the floor! That was the only hole we had to patch in the ceiling. We had a yard light to turn on with a switch on the meter pole and lights and plug ins in the garage.

We did not have water except a cistern with the pitcher pump, so we still had the little 'outhouse'. The thing was, we needed electrical appliances such as a refrigerator, toaster, etc. We soon had a refrigerator so we could now have ice and keep the milk cold. This had to be one of my most fond remembrances in my life. We also got a propane heater that heated the house except for the bedrooms.

Dad bought a used 1946 Ford pickup that the gas company in Lamar had traded in for a new one. It was in very good shape. He and Mom had a dependable vehicle now to ride ditch with.

I bought a used 1941 Ford two door sedan that had the second gear out of the transmission. The previous owner's wife was real short and did not get the clutch all the way in when she shifted it into second gear. It was at the Ray Chevrolet Company in Lamar. They wanted two hundred and twenty-five dollars for it but said if I would take it like it was I could buy it for one hundred and eighty-five dollars. It cost me five dollars for a used second gear, which I installed myself. Ted also bought a 1941 Ford that same time. We were two happy seniors going into school that fall.

Just before school started I wanted to take a trip in my 1941 Ford. I took Mother and Granddad and Grandma Clark to Arkansas to visit Russell and Martha Ohlson. I dropped Granddad and Grandma off at Chautaqua, Kansas where they had lived before moving to Colorado. I picked them back up on our return trip from Arkansas. They spent the week with some old friends. I remember my Grandma going up to their house and jokingly telling the woman that she was selling magazines. It took a while for this old time friend to recognize Grandma.

While we were at Ohlson's in Arkansas, we all drove to Fayetteville where Mother was born and lived until she moved to Colorado with her Grandmother Bentley. We also went to the McDowell Cemetery at Vale, just south of Fayetteville. Mom's Granddad, Aunts and her parents, the Keeler's are all buried there, just a few miles from their old home place in Arkansas.

Granddad and Grandma Clark moved to the larger house they owned closer to downtown. It had three bedrooms upstairs and two bedrooms downstairs. It really worked out better for them because Grandma could walk to Church and Granddad could walk downtown to go to school (as he called it). He would meet some of his older men friends down on the street corner by the Corner Pharmacy and talk. If the weather was bad they would go to the pool hall to visit.

This house had an upstairs bedroom that had a bed with a feather mattress. I stayed there even when I was out of high school and was out late. It was like having my own room in town.

While in my senior year I still did quite a bit of welding. I helped Jack Good rebuild his 1934 Plymouth engine. I also helped Lawrence Flint overhaul his 1938 Chevy convertible engine. I also overhauled my car as well as Ted's.

A lot of my time was also spent on building a boat. Gary Coen decided to build a full size boat. I was a close friend to Gary so I wanted to be a part of this project. Gary was real good with the wood part of the construction and I would help with whatever I could. We worked on that boat every minute we could. We both entered the district contest as the farm mechanics team and won. This competition was the ag classes in the Arkansas Valley schools. We went to Fort Collins to enter the state contest. I thought we might really be in trouble as the state divided the farm mechanics contest into two separate classes. One of us would draw welding, both arc and gas welding with drill bit sharpening; while the other one would have all soldering and wood working, cutting rafters, etc. I knew if I got the woodworking I would not do well and Gary knew if he got the welding part he would likewise not do well. We were lucky, we got just what we wanted, Gary with the woods and me with the welding. We won the State competition on the farm mechanics. I have that trophy in my possession as Gary was killed some years later. I was a member of the Lamar School Board and told the present Ag Teacher at that time what that trophy meant to me. He took it out of the case at the High School and said "it's yours to keep".

We completed the boat. We even water skied behind it, but due to the weight of the boat, we needed a much larger engine. However, it did pull one of us at a time on water skies.

One evening Ruth, Mary Lou, Ted and I thought some homemade ice cream would really be good. We had our own milk, cream and eggs, but it was May and there was no ice on the lakes. I had an idea that might work for ice. Mary Lou and I went west of the house two miles to the Santana ditch that ran water into the lakes. We had a huge ice jam there the last time water ran there in March. We had some heavy blowing dirt storms after that and the blow dirt had drifted into the ditch over the ice. We took a shovel, axe and a gunny sack and made our way to the bottom of the ditch. We scooped blow dirt away about two feet deep. There it was, all the ice we needed. I took the axe and chopped about thirty pounds of ice loose and put it in the gunny sack. After the ice cream was churned and we all had some of it, no one thought our idea was just a fantasy.

In my last year of Ag and FFA, the State had a competition in Parliamentary Procedure. Our Lamar FFA Chapter had a very good team, but there was another school that always beat us and we would wind up in second place. This happened for about three years in a row. I was part of this team. We would have mock meetings using all the procedures of amendments, motions, correct those out of order, etc. Hecklers had been trained to trip you. For example they would say "I move we buy a horse". There was already a motion on the floor that had nothing to do with a horse. The President would tell that person they were out of order and why.

I had already decided that I was not going out of town to attend college and would stay around Lamar. I found out I could remain in FFA one more year after graduation. I stayed in the FFA for a fifth year and wanted to pursue the parliamentary procedure team to win that year at the State competition.

I was acting as President on our team. We had meetings during the summer to practice. With the help of all the others on the team, I was sure we would have a great chance at winning. Roberts Rules of Order was what we all read and read and read! We practiced doing all the things that hecklers would be doing in the actual contest. We won in the end, winning First Place. That finalized my year in FFA.

Chapter Six

I went to work full time for the Amity in 1954. My pay scale advanced to one dollar an hour which was about twenty-five cents an hour more than the going wage. Clyde Shelton was operating the dragline and started training me to operate it. I would operate it for one to two hours a day. Clyde was in his 60's and enjoyed the break from operating the machine. The dry weather along with a lot of wind had filled a lot of the lake ditches. Also the east part of the Amity canal that carried water for irrigation to the farmers was full of blow dirt. I was kept busy with the bulldozer pushing dirt out of the canal.

Clyde went on to work for the City of Lamar. The Lima dragline needed lots of work on it. It was on tracks and would only go about a half mile an hour if you needed to move it. The Amity Board purchased a new Bantam dragline in 1955 and I was to run it. I also did most of the dozer work but they would have someone hired to operate the dozer when we needed extra help.

This was how my employment was to continue, with me still living at home at the lakes. I could continue to help my parents with the livestock and also financially. I bought a 1952 Ford pickup so I could use it on the ditch job. Gas was furnished for it. I also used the pickup for chasing around.

I did not have a serious girlfriend at the time but would date different girls mostly from Church. I was active in the youth group at First Baptist Church.

Ted worked that summer then went to Fort Collins to attend college. He studied Entomology and was in the R.O.T.C. program. After his graduation he made a career of the Air Force as an officer.

My friend, Gary Coen did not go off to college either, so we ran around together all the time. Gary joined the Baptist Church and we attended all the B.Y.F. parties. We would also goose hunt in the winter. We dug pits and would sit in there freezing before daylight just to shoot a goose! We thought we would freeze to death.

The following story of goose hunting has to be the most stupid, dangerous thing I ever did in my life.

Gary and I were trying to hide out close to the Upper Queen Lake to shoot our geese, but when they came off to go feed they were flying high, too far out to hit them. We decided to take a white sheet, go out on the ice a ways and cover up with the sheet. This would put us close enough to get a goose. Well, it was real foggy that morning. We went out quite a ways on the lake, but still could not see the geese as they were flying. Geese and ducks always kept a spot in the middle of a lake stirred up to where there would remain water that would not freeze. When the fog lifted that morning all the geese had left the open water, but there were some ducks out there.

We decided we would walk up as close as we could and shoot some ducks. Now, we both had a lot of clothing on as it was really cold. We had coveralls, coats, gloves, and fur caps so we were fully dressed with all this outer wear. We got close enough that we shot several ducks on the open water area. The light breeze pushed them to the edge of the ice. The water was probably thirty feet deep below us. We got on our hands and knees, crawled up to the edge, reached over and picked up the ducks. Why that ice did not break off at the edge by the water was only one reason, I'm sure. Our guardian angel must have said "I'll give you one more chance, but you are both old enough to know that if that ice had broken with all the clothes you have on, you would both have drowned immediately".

We did a lot of jack rabbit hunting at night. We would shoot as many as forty or fifty in one night. They were so thick that there was an outfit that was buying them to make dog food, etc. out of them. We could get ten or fifteen cents a rabbit for them. I remember taking in a bunch in to the north part of Lamar to sell and there were at least a thousand rabbits brought in from all over southeast Colorado to sell.

One time Gary and I had been driving the Kicking Bird canal road north of Hasty looking for a coyote to shoot. We noticed an eagle that was crippled with one wing that would not allow it to fly. It was by itself on the prairie. Gary ran out and caught it, one hand on its head and the other holding its feet. I asked him "what in the world are you going to do now?" He said "I'm taking it home and putting it out in the feedlot with the cows so it can heal". I asked him "how are you taking it home?" He said "in the car with us". I told him either I was going to walk or else he would have to hold that eagle in the back seat while I drove his car. He opted to hold the eagle himself. I drove and we took that eagle to his Dad and Uncle's feedlot next to their house. That eagle stayed on the feedlot fence to itself. Gary made sure there was a dead jack rabbit close by for it to feed on. It got well enough that after several weeks, it flew off.

I had been driving Ford pickups. They had been fairly new ones in good shape. However, when you wanted to take your date and another couple with you, it was too crowded. Plus I always had a fuel tank in the back and lots of tools. That was not the best for leaving it on the street while you were at the movies. One of my friends had traded his 1940 Plymouth for a really good low mileage 1949 Chevrolet. I knew his old Plymouth had a good body, was a sedan and would work good for a car to run around in. It, however, used lots of oil, but of course I could overhaul it if I decided to want to use it for more than a chase around car. One evening it was cold, really cold, about zero degrees. I went outside to start it to let it run for a while to charge up the battery to keep it from freezing. It would not start, which was normal for it. It never started very easy if it was hot, or if it was cold. Just the way Chrysler products were at that time. I got Mary Lou to come out and push it with my pickup. I left it running and went back into the house. After about twenty minutes I decided it was time to shut it off, so I dashed out of the house without a coat. I was dressed in a tee shirt and jeans. There was no need for a coat, hat or gloves just to turn off the key and run back to the house. Everyone else had gone to bed or was doing their own thing. When I ran out to the car, I jumped in it. The heater had been left on. It was quite warm and cozy, especially since it was below zero. I decided to drive down the road a ways before shutting it off and going back in the house. That was my first mistake. My second mistake was turning around about halfway to the Gentz place which was two miles from home and two miles to their place. The car died on me when I was in the process of turning around. It was about

9:30 at night. I had no other clothes in the car. I could see car lights several miles in the distance down the May Valley road I was on. I thought that when the car got there I would get a push or ride back home. Well, the car turned off the main road. By then I was really getting cold. I tried to push it, then jump in, put it in gear and start it. On a gravel road that was flat, that did not work. I then decided I had better high tail it home as quick as I could. I started north. There was a brisk north wind and at that temperature it was too much for me. I went just a little way, then ran back to the car. I couldn't warm up in there but I was out of the wind. I thought there was only one other thing to do and that was to run south with the wind to my back and go to Gentz's. I got to their house pretty quick, as I ran practically all the way. I banged on the door. Mrs. Gentz, Louise Gentz, Roy Hufford and Edna Hufford were all playing pitch. They looked really surprised as I came charging into the house just in a white tee shirt and no coat. Their thermometer showed ten degrees below zero! After explaining my predicament to them and warming up, Roy took their pickup and gave me a push then followed me on home. At that time I was so mad at that Plymouth I vowed to never own another Chrysler product. I took the motor out of that Plymouth and sold it to somebody. I then drove the bulldozer over that Plymouth and to this day fifty some years later the mashed Plymouth remains where I left it, next to some trees and other old junk by the lower Queen Lake. AMEN.

We had lots of ice skating parties on the lake in the winter. It was fun to have a date and take her skating. We would build a fire on the ice to roast hot dogs and make hot chocolate. If it had snowed we would make paths and play fox and geese.

Jack Good had stayed in Lamar after graduation before going to a four year college. He attended Lamar Junior College. He would usually join us at the ice skating parties.

Jack married Berna Kay Turpin and Cecil Piper married Gail Heath as soon as the girls graduated. Gail and Berna Kay were very close to me as friends. I had gone to grade school with both of them. Gail and I would attend school dances together, not as one would think as dating, but if neither one of us were dating anyone at the time, we would go together. That way we were not single at the dance. After their marriages that still left Gary and I to run around together as we were both not dating anyone seriously.

Ted came home for Christmas break from his first year in college. We had our cows close to the Upper Queen as the Lower Queen was about dry from the drought. We both went up to the lake to chop ice for the cows to drink. There were geese pretty close to shore, about fifty yards out. Mike, our bird dog was crazy about hunting and immediately ran out towards them on the ice. He fell through the ice and could not get back upon it. Ted and I knew it was over our heads, so we did not know what to do. I told Ted that Perdue's had a small aluminum boat if I could go after it and get back in time to save Mike. I took off, but it had snowed and blew in the night. The road had some big drifts in it. However, with much speed and determination I was able to plow on thru the snow. I got their boat and back to the lake I went. It probably took me about twenty minutes. When I returned Mike was still in the ice water paddling away. Ted and I thought "we made it". We grabbed a hold of the boat and started pushing it on the ice towards Mike. We got within about twenty-five feet of Mike when we both broke through the ice. We were able to climb aboard the little boat. Ted had an axe and was breaking the ice ahead of the boat as we approached Mike. About ten feet from him, he just quit paddling and I guess his heart gave out. We were to him in less than two minutes. We got him in the boat and tried everything we knew how to do to try to revive him but we were not able to save him. It was very hard to go home and tell Dad what had happened. Mike was around thirteen years old and had been special to all of us. He was a good retriever for ducks, geese, pheasants and rabbits. He was also good at killing rattlesnakes. He had been bitten on the face one time by a rattlesnake but with some medicine from the Vet, he lived through that. If we were going hunting and had a gun in our hand standing around, Mike would go up to the barrel of the gun and take it in his mouth and tug on it and try to hurry us up. When Uncle Fred, Uncle Ralph or any of our friends and relatives came up to hunt they always wanted Mike to go with them to either retrieve or else sniff out pheasants in the weed patches or other cover they would hide in.

One late winter evening, for some unknown reason, I decided to check the cows just before dark. They were grazing about three-fourths of a mile west of the ditch house on the west side of the Lower Queen dike. As I was about to turn around and drive back home, I thought I noticed a person on west of where I was, just standing in the grass pasture. I drove towards the person. When I got to him, I recognized him. It was Mr. Bear. He and his wife lived in Lamar and both were handicapped. He used one crutch and she used a walker. They liked to go for drives in the country quite often out our way around the lakes.

When I drove up to Mr. Bear, I said "what in the world are you doing out here on foot"? He said "my wife and I went on a drive this morning and we decided to drive on west to go over to Highway 287 and see something different". There were no roads, just pasture trails where he had tried to go. He said "I got stuck in blow sand and could not get out". "I left my wife at the car and was trying to go back to your place and I just can't go anymore". I got him in my pickup and headed back towards his car which was about three and a half miles from where I picked him up. He was exhausted from struggling to walk with the help of his one crutch. When we got close to the car, there was his wife using her walker about one hundred yards from the car. She was worried, confused and disoriented after being in the car all afternoon. Thank goodness the temperature was not below freezing. I'm sure my guardian angel must have said "Keith, I have helped you enough, now it's your turn to help someone". It could have been several days before anyone might have driven to where they were stuck. I was able to pull him out of the sand with my pickup and get him back on the road.

Gary Coen had a sister, Nona who was three years younger than me. Nona had a good friend in her class by the name of Louise Bever. I knew who Louise was as she was a freshman when I was a senior in high school. I remember she had an afternoon class on the lower level of the high school where the Ag classroom was located. She seemed always to be getting a drink at the water fountain on down the hallway right after the noon recess. She had long hair and I thought she was sure a pretty girl, but I did not know her personally.

In the summer of 1956, Gary had a date with Louise. I was

not going with anyone at the time so I asked Nona for a date and we double dated. It was August and we went to the John Martin Dam and had a picnic at Lake Hasty. We drove on into Las Animas and just rode around. This let me get to know Louise as we had a good time just the four of us out riding around.

As the summer went on, I took Mother and Mary Lou to Wyoming in my pickup. We visited the Keeler's in Farson and then drove on to Star Valley where Goldie and DeVerle were living. We went on to Pocatello, Idaho and visited Rayma and Elmer. Elmer was working for the railroad. All the time we were on this trip my pickup was not starting very easy the first thing in the morning. It was September and much cooler there than at home. I knew the engine had lots of miles on it and needed an overhaul.

After returning home, I decided to buy a brand new pickup. On October 1, 1956 I bought a new pickup. It was a baby blue color with a V-8 motor.

I knew Gary was not dating Louise so I thought maybe since we had made our acquaintance earlier in the summer, she might consider going out with me. After all, I did have a brand new Ford less than a week old. I called her on the telephone and she accepted a date with me to go to a teen dance on Saturday, October 5th. We had a good time at the dance and from then on we dated a lot. Mostly we went to the movies.

Louise and I continued to see each other, but did not go steady. Louise was active in her church, the First Christian Church, and I was active in the First Baptist Church where we had a youth group for college age youth. She attended the college youth group with me.

On March 23, 1957, Sunday afternoon, we were riding around together and I asked her to go steady with me and she accepted. From then on, we were going out as often as she was permitted. Louise was a senior in high school and very involved in the school plays, pep club and other various activities, so we had to accept that we could not be together every night. Saturday nights and Sunday night youth group we were usually together.

July 4, 1957 I took Louise, my cousin Ruth and her husband, Noel King on a long day trip. We all four loaded into my pickup and went to Colorado Springs, Manitou and up to the top of Pikes Peak. When I took Louise home that evening, her mother told me she had some real bad news to tell me. Earl Gentz was hit by a train In Sheridan Lake, Colorado and was killed. This was really a shock as Earl was one of my closet friends ever since we had moved to the lakes.

Earl was married and had two small daughters. He worked for an alfalfa dehydrating company and was moving back east with the company for the summer season. His wife was in the car behind him that early morning. The train was coming from the East with the sun just coming up. He evidently did not see the train. He had the company tractor on the truck he was driving. When the train hit it, the tractor exploded, killing both engineers and Earl.

I was kept busy that summer with my job as the heavy equipment operator. We had a big rain that washed out about thirteen places in the canal. I also had rented one hundred and sixty acres of farm land with Uncle Ralph.

October was soon approaching. Louise and I had our first date almost a year earlier and had been going steady for six months. She had a part-time job at a loan company and was also attending Lamar Junior College. I decided to ask her Dad if I could marry her. He said he would be proud to have me for a son-in-law. We became engaged on October 5th, exactly one year from our first date. We bought candied apples to eat and it is traditional now that every year on October 5th we share a candied apple! We planned to marry in June 1958.

I had a 1951 Ford V-8 car at this time. It was a good, dependable vehicle. I left it in town at Louise's parent's house after we were engaged. She drove it to college and to work. They had a two car garage so it was garaged. When we went out, I could park the pickup and we used the car.

Soon after our engagement, my friend Roy Hufford, who lived with the Gentz family and also work for them, became engaged to their daughter, Louise Gentz. She was a classmate of my Louise. I had worked for John Gentz off and on before I was out of high school. Earl, Roy and I ran around together, rabbit hunting, working on old cars, fishing, etc. After Earl was killed, Roy and I still did some things together. After my engagement, and also Roy's, I stopped at May Valley Store and Roy was there. He had just purchased a 1951 Ford car also. We discussed our cars and visited for some time before we left the store. Roy was working at the Big Bend Hay Mill as a mechanic and handyman. That is where my cousin, Gilbert Gaydon had worked when he lived with us. He was also a friend to Roy. About a week after visiting with Roy at the store we had a drizzly day. Roy was welding some iron outside the mill shop. Somehow, he got a hold of a high voltage cable and was electrocuted. This was a very sad thing to happen as Earl and Roy were both gone within six months of each other. Two good friends were now gone.

Louise and I were at her parents quite a bit when we were together. We were busy planning our wedding getting ready to order the wedding invitations. We both had lots of relatives and friends in each of our churches.

That Christmas I gave Louise a pair of ice skates and she gave me a very nice yellow sweater. We skated quite a bit as it was a cold winter and the ice was thick.

Right after the first of the year I traded my 1956 Pickup for a new 1958 model. It was a two-tone custom cab and was really a good looking pickup. I had the same job I had grown up with, operating the heavy equipment for the ditch company, so my job was secure. Soon after buying the pickup the Kiowa County Board of Selective Service notified me by certified mail to go to Denver to take my physical for the Army. Gary Coen was in the Colorado National Guards, so he was not worried about being drafted. I thought that since Kiowa County did not have any industry and most young men my age would probably volunteer for the draft, I would probably not be called up. Therefore, I did not join the National Guard.

Louise and I continued to make plans to marry in June. Mr. Wissell, the head of the Kiowa County Selective Service was also a barber. I went up to Eads to talk to him and also get a haircut. He assured me that they would need to fill their quota before very long, but he would be able to hold off for a few months. That would allow us to get married before entering the Army.

Louise and I decided to move the date up to April 20th. There was much to do with the short time left before April. One was that I had better sell that new pickup and buy an older one to use until I was actually drafted. Another thing I needed to take care of was the crop Uncle Ralph and I had. We thought we had the variety of feed that would be grain that only grew about four feet high. The seed had been miss-tagged and we had planted atlas sargo, which grew to about six or seven feet high. We decided to bind it into bundle feed and we hired it cut and shocked. The market was not good in the fall and we were only offered about twelve dollars per ton. We needed more than that to break even. We held it over during the winter. We needed to sell that feed. We were able to sell it to someone who put cattle on pasture next to our field.

We also needed to make plans to find an apartment or house to live in. My Aunt Gussie had died a short time before and her house was still empty. It needed painted inside and the bedroom could use new wallpaper. Louise and I painted in the evenings and her parents wallpapered the bedroom. They had previous experience with wallpapering and were good at it. Her Mother also sewed drapes for the front room.

On Saturday, April 19, the day before our wedding, a man bought the new pickup but did not want to wait a week until we returned from our honeymoon. We decided to not leave right after the wedding but to wait until Monday morning. That would allow me to go to the bank to make the transaction.

It was a beautiful day when our wedding took place in the First Christian Church. It was packed with friends and relatives. My grandmother Clark and Louise's grandmother Bever were there and that was special to both of us.

After the ceremony and reception, we took off in the '51

Ford. There was writing all over the car and tin cans tied to the bumper making noise as we were chased down Main Street and out of town. We went to La Junta for dinner and a movie but returned to Lamar that night because of the pickup. As soon as the papers were signed, I went to the Ford Garage. They had just taken in a 1948 Ford pickup on trade. I made a deal to buy it contingent on new paint. They agreed. It would be ready when we returned from our honeymoon. Somehow this pickup got named 'Clancy' and we had it for many years even after I purchased new ones. Clancy was around for farm use. Our kids even learned to drive it.

We stopped in Springfield for lunch at the Main Café. We had decided to go south, clear to Mexico on our honeymoon. We would go to Juarez, Mexico and circle to the west through Santa Fe and back home all in a week's time.

Back home and back to work for both of us. In this era of time there was always a chivaree for newlyweds. Jim Labertew was the ramrod of this. I had figured out he would be, so I called him one day and pretended to be Noel King. He said they had it planned for a certain evening. We could shut the door to the kitchen and lock it. That meant when we locked the door, our friends would not be able to remove the labels from our canned goods. We were prepared, the cigars, sodas and candy were all purchased. When we were picked up, our friends had borrowed a heavy ball and chain from the sheriff's office. It was locked on to my ankle and my bride was put in a wheelbarrow for me to push her all the way up Main Street. That started at Mickey's Grocery in the 400 block of north main and ended in the 400 block of south Main Street, including the distance of one block over the train tracks for a total of nine blocks. We then returned to our house where we had the treats waiting and had a great time together.

In the latter part of May a letter arrived telling me to go to Eads, take the train to Denver and be processed into the army on June 25th. The Amity hired a man for me to train to operate the dragline before I left.

It was early in the morning when Louise dropped me off in Eads. She returned to Lamar and I was on my way to Denver via Pueblo on the train. I was processed the next day, and then put on a bus with a group of other inductees for Fort Carson.

We were put in a group with about one hundred and twenty other soldiers. We were given haircuts and assigned to a company. After arriving at the company we were issued clothes and boots along with our rifle and canteens and assigned to a platoon. There was to be eight weeks of basic training. There had been about five days already behind us. Then we had a zero week while the company was filled to its quota. That made about two full weeks when we started our first week of count.

Marvin Hasser had already been in the service and was discharged when I went in. He was selected to the Honor Guard in Washington D.C., an honorable assignment. Marvin told me I should take my hair clippers with me and I could probably cut hair and get out of details on Friday nights when everyone else was scrubbing and cleaning the barracks. I had cut hair at home for Dad, Ted and Gilbert. I took my clippers along. When we were issued army clothes we were forced to bag up our civilian clothes and send everything home. Only army issued articles were to be in our foot lockers. I thought I might really get into trouble keeping the clippers out of site if I was caught, but I kept them anyhow. Every morning there were some soldiers that were selected for trash duty and various jobs that were not pleasant. I had not been in any trouble and had not been picked on. Once you were it seemed like they would choose you again. You made a name for yourself that was not good.

The first Friday morning our platoon sergeant had us in formation and was telling us that in the evening we would be doing all the cleaning for an inspection on Saturday morning and he expected us to be the best. Before he dismissed us, he asked "Is there anyone here that cuts hair"? I did not know whether to answer or not. He blurted out again, "Is there anybody here that can give haircuts"? I answered, "Yes, sir, I can". I wondered what I might be getting myself. Perhaps I should have kept my mouth shut. But I remembered what Marvin had told me so I took a chance. The sergeant looked at me, "Do you have your hair clippers with you"? I nodded, "Yes sir". He asked "Can you give everyone in this platoon a haircut?" That was sixty soldiers. I answered and told him I might not be able to cut that many in one evening. He looked at me and said "if I told you I could cut that many, do you think you could"? I answered, "yes sir". He then told everyone in the formation that I would give each one a haircut and I would cut it as close as my clippers would cut it everywhere on the head. He said I could not charge them but he told everyone they had better leave a quarter after the haircut. He also told me that after the first week, on the next Friday night I could just cut the sides close and that would allow the top to grow out a little. He also told me I could use a small room that was located at the beginning of the barracks on the second floor where my area was and I was not expected to do any cleaning. I was just the barber on Friday nights.

This let me get out of cleaning on that first Friday night and also meant I could make twelve dollars, which I used in the pay phone to call home to Louise. One other plus was that I was known to the sergeant and never drew any of the details that were given out to some of the goof offers. (Thanks, Marvin).

I made friends with the other recruits. Most were from Texas and Minnesota. They were different from each other. I made good friends with some from Oklahoma and the Texas panhandle, more like us Colorado people. One guy from Oklahoma, Gene Barker, had a wife that drove up to Fort Carson at the same time Louise was able to come up. Our wives met and Gene's wife, Jeanette, stayed with Louise in Lamar for several weeks. That made it possible for her to come up more often to see both of us. When basic training was completed, we graduated to the second part of our training. Most of the group was sent on to Korea. I and about six others had our orders held up. We spent an extra week there after the others were gone. When my orders came in, I was put into artillery. I had some time off, about two weeks before reporting into the new unit. While on leave at home, Louise and I bought a twenty-seven foot trailer and we pulled it back to Colorado Springs and put it in a trailer park. We also learned by this time that Louise was pregnant with our first child. The baby was due in March. I could not live off base at the trailer park but I could get some passes quite often and could go down to the PX in the evenings and call Louise on the telephone. I enjoyed the artillery. We trained on the 105 Howitzer guns. We practiced taking them apart until we could do it with our eyes shut. We pulled them out in the field with the two and a half ton army trucks. The first time we shot one off I was not prepared for the amount of noise they made. I think we had a charge five in the projectile. When a charge seven was in the howitzer it could shoot upwards of six miles. When we were set up for the practice I got the job of taking an officer out to the lookout point. There were some old tanks about five miles from the guns that were parked in the field. Our position let us observe where the projectile hit. We were trying to zero in on the old deserted tanks. We would report by our observation which way and about how far the hit was from the tanks. There was another team that would figure how much to raise or lower the howitzer and shoot again. One time we were lucky enough to hit a tank head on. That was not always the objective as hitting close could cause an explosive projectile that would kill the enemy with shrapnel, etc.

I had been issued a driver's license for both the two and a half ton trucks plus the little jeep.

When I had been in the infantry in basic training on one of our ten mile hikes, my right knee started giving me a lot of pain. I did not dare go on sick call to the doctor for fear that I might leave my unit long enough to be recycled. I sure did not want to start all over in basic with another unit. After I was in artillery I thought maybe I would have my knee checked out. I was not having any trouble now that I drove the trucks and jeeps out in the field. The army doctor examined my knee and said I had some loose tendons letting my leg bend sideways somewhat. This did not bother me, however he said "I'll put this in your medical records that you have a Class C profile of the right knee.

Chapter Seven

We were almost through with the artillery training. Payday was your name being called off in alphabetical order and your check issued. My name was skipped. After all the names were read, I went to the sergeant to see what was wrong. He sent me to the payroll officer. He looked through some papers and said "oh, yes, you are being transferred out of here. I knew nothing of this and wondered what would happen as Louise was living in Colorado Springs at the WWW Trailer Court. In about three days I was sent over to personnel where they told me I was to be assigned to range control at the Fort Carson Base.

This seemed like a placement I would like as I was allowed to live off base. I would report to duty each day Monday thru Friday. I was one of six that was placed into that job. Everyone had been taken from the unit they were in because of some physical impairment. Most of the others were from vision while mine stemmed back to my knee. At first we were helping civilians that were responsible for making targets. Since I had a driver's license, I was soon singled out to drive a Lieutenant all over the base checking where soldiers were on shooting ranges. We more or less just drove around. I did not mind that at all. One of the other six was Homer Kirk, who was from Oklahoma. His wife, Annie was from the same area and was also in Colorado Springs living in an apartment. We became friends with them. About one week before Christmas we all got orders to go to Fort Huachuca, Arizona. We had never heard of the place. It was a Combat Development Base that at one time had been an all black military calvary base. It had been re-opened and was in the process of being actively re-organized. I could not find anyone who knew much about housing there. Since it was doubtful that there would be anywhere for our little trailer it was decided to park it in Louise's parents backyard and hook onto the water, sewer and electricity. She could live there and I would drive on to Fort Huachuca. I had to report in the first Monday of January 1959. I arranged to pick up Delbert Gaston in Amarillo, Texas. He was from Norman, Oklahoma. I also picked up Homer Kirk in Lubbock, Texas. They were also two of the six of us that had been together at Fort Carson. It was below zero the day I left Lamar. I allowed two days to drive there. After picking up Delbert and Homer we took turns driving and sleeping in the car. We arrived early afternoon on Sunday before we were to report in on Monday morning. The small town to the very east edge of Fort Huachuca was Fry, Arizona but was changing its name to Sierra Vista. It was full of trailers in trailer parks and also lots of apartments to rent. They were not much to live in as most were made out of old army barracks.

I was assigned to the motor pool. All the others were placed in other parts of the base. Delbert went to the Airport on Fort Huachuca. Homer went to the field assigned signal communications. I was given a test to obtain a drivers license for buses, shuttle buses and all sizes of army vehicles. I had no trouble at all. The Sergeant in charge of testing me looked over to an old Ford truck with a flat bed. It was a ton and a half that had an old four speed transmission. They were not easy to shift. You needed to double clutch them unless you were really used to them. He was kinda cocky and said "well, let's see what you can do now"? He did not know that I grew up on those old types of shifting gears. We got in it and I drove off, with not a hint of any gear grinding. He looked dumbfounded then I told him I was a farm boy and had driven about everything. After that I was shown a map with three different bus routes on base and one that went off base to Sierra Vista. The routes each took about twenty-five minutes to complete. They were called the yellow, blue and red route. Each had a certain route. Civilians could ride the buses also. It was a free ride. The other duty was a passenger car that was like a taxi cab. It was for certain military use only. They had to call dispatch who would then radio a cab to be picked up. You then sat at that drop off location until the dispatcher sent you on another assignment.

By this time I could see this was where I would probably stay the rest of my military service time. Now I needed to get Louise down there but did not have any leave time to go after her. I located a small two room apartment. By two rooms, I mean a small bedroom and a small kitchen/living room. It was smaller than our first Casa Manana trailer, but it would mean Louise and I could be together. I think the rent was sixty five dollars a month. I checked and found out that Louise could catch a train in Lamar with one transfer in Albuquerque. She would get off at Bisbee Junction, located about a mile north of Mexico. She was to arrive there at 3:00 a.m. after nearly a two day trip. The apartment was rented and I made the necessary arrangements for off base living and the train schedule was in place. Homer went with me to Bisbee. We went to a movie, sat through it a second time, then about midnight drove to Bisbee Junction to wait for the train. There was not anything else around except the train depot which did not amount to much. The train was on time. It was pitch dark out but a beautiful sight to once again see and be reunited with my bride of less than a year. She was definitely pregnant as it was the latter part of January and the baby was due the middle of March.

Back to the apartment I took her. The long hallway led to separate men and women's bathrooms that were shared with other tenants. The only heat was from the oven on the cook stove. Homer wanted Annie down there also. We found a seventy foot trailer that we could rent together and we knew that Louise and Annie would do just great living as one family together. Homer's Dad brought Annie down with their car and took the bus back to Oklahoma.

Louise would sometimes walk to the edge of Sierra Vista to the main gate of the Fort. If I was driving that bus route on that particular day, she would ride the bus with me the last hour until it was time to end my tour. It was only about two blocks from our residence to the gate.

One morning when I checked in at the motor pool the Sergeant said "Clark, you report to the General's Office across the street from the Headquarters building". I thought "oh boy, what have I done now"? I went into the office where there was a retired Major at a desk. I identified myself. He said to have a seat, the Colonel would be in soon. I still had no idea what was going on. After some stillness in the room, the Major said "Clark, are you a farm boy?". I said "yes sir". He then said uh huh real slow about two times. I thought "I'll bet you are going to have me dig a flower bed or a garden plot". The Colonel came in. His office desk was next to the commanding General's desk in this part of the building. I was a little nervous, but I was here, not any way to change anything, but just say my Yes Sirs and No Sirs.

After an introduction to the Colonel, he also asked me that same question, "Clark, are you a farm boy?" By this time I was sure I would be handed a shovel and rake to go do yard work. Colonel Moynahan said "let's go for a drive". I had been given a 1957 Chevrolet with just a few miles on it to drive that day. It was the usual army vehicle, three speed standard transmission.

Colonel Moynahan asked me to drive him to a place on base. I did as I was asked. He soon told me that I was just who he had asked for, a farm boy that could drive a car with a clutch, not jerk it on starts and not grind gears. His last driver was a city boy who had never learned to drive a stick shift. This was the beginning of a very special enlisted soldier and a Colonel who was just under the General at Fort Huachuca. From there on it was a very happy assignment for me. I was assigned the 1957 Chevrolet and I was allowed to keep it in an enclosed two car garage with the commanding General's car. This made it easy for me to keep the car clean and waxed.

After we moved to the trailer house it was quite an improvement over the apartment. We now had room for both couples and room for company. Louise was put in the hospital March 1st and they induced labor. Her parents arrived, but no baby yet. She was released from the hospital after a few days. We even drove over into Naco, Mexico for a day. Finally, on March 10th, labor began. The Doctor at Fort Huachuca said for me to go home and sleep and call about 5:00 a.m. the next morning. I did so and found out that Rodney Keith was born at 4:00 a.m. that morning. We had this name picked for a long time and the name Pamela Lynn if it was a girl. After a few days Louise and Rod were released from the hospital. Mary Ellen, Louise's mother, paid the ten dollars it cost for the hospital bill. Mary Ellen always said Rod was hers as she paid for him! After her parents went back home, we had lots of help with Homer and Annie living in the same home with us.

The motor in my 1951 Ford needed an overhaul. I could do the work myself except I did not have a hoist to remove the engine and would have to find a machine shop to grind the valves. I checked with a salvage yard at Huachuca City, just north of the army base. They had just received a wrecked car that had a good running flat head Ford engine in it. I bought it for seventy five dollars with the agreement to use a hoist for a few days. I took off my trunk lid, had the salvage yard load the motor into my trunk. That was on a Friday evening. Early that Saturday morning Homer and I drove east of town on the San Pedro River where we found a big cottonwood tree. We backed up to the tree, hooked the hoist on a large limb about ten feet off of the ground. We unloaded the newly acquired motor. Then we turned the car around, drove under the tree and removed the old motor. We had only one set of open wrenches and a socket set. We exchanged the motors and had a can to catch the fluid out of the radiator. We started the car and drove back to the trailer in Sierra Vista all before noon. I don't think today's cars would let us do all that in such a short amount of time. We did not even take Homer's car out there for a back-up. That motor served me well from there on.

We played lots of cards in the evenings. We had no television, so entertainment was visiting and games. The General's driver and his wife often came over and joined in on canasta with us.

Just before Mother's Day in May, Louise and I along with Homer and Annie met Louise's parents and my Dad and Mom in Carrizozo, New Mexico. That was about four hundred miles for each of us to drive. My parents had not met Rod yet. We had a picnic lunch together then my Mother came home with us to stay a week. She returned to Lamar by bus. I mentioned to Colonel Moynahan that my Mother was visiting. He said "what are you doing here?" "I don't have anything going on that you have to be here". I had the next several days off. I was not required to report in and did not have parade duty or any of that. I always drove the Colonel to such events and was entirely his responsibility. Sometimes I would run errands for his secretary. Other times I drove to Tucson to pick up people that were flying into Arizona for meetings with the Colonel and the General.

One day we were driving around Sierra Vista and noticed a car with Colorado license plates. The letters on the plate started with W G. That was Baca County, just south of Prowers County. We followed that car until it stopped by a little tiny trailer in a trailer court full of older, small trailers. This couple got out of their car and we pulled up behind them. We introduced ourselves to them and told them where we were from. They were Randall and Mary Martin from Springfield, Colorado. We immediately started talking. Randall had graduated the same year as I and we soon found we both knew some of the same people. An immediate friendship developed. We also discovered we both owned trailers of the same make. We talked about getting our own trailers down there and possibly renting a lot together to park them on. A search began for a place to park the trailers. We found a full size lot with a lawn, storage shed and electric and sewer hook-up. It was plenty big enough for both trailers and still have a large yard. The owner said we could rent it and split the rent and utilities between us.

Louise and I were going back to Colorado in July to attend Mary Lou's wedding. I had leave coming. Randall did not have any extra time to take off to go after his trailer. We talked about how to get his trailer there. We decided that the 4th of July weekend he would be free Saturday, Sunday and Monday. Could we drive to Colorado and back within these three days? Randall studied the map real close and said "I think it will all work except just past Alamogordo there is a mountain pass that I do not think my car will pull my trailer". He had a 1952 Ford flathead like my '51, but his trailer was longer than ours, thirty five feet instead of twenty seven feet long like ours. I said if we took our '51 and left it set in Alamogordo, we could hook the two cars together and over the mountain we could go. We could leave Friday night and drive all night and get to Springfield early Saturday morning, spend the day, then leave early Sunday and drive all day and night. We would have part of Monday to make the trip, barring no trouble, of course.

This short trip would allow Louise to stay in Lamar for a week so the grandparents could have more time with Rod. We would bring Randall's mother and his younger brother, Ken back to Arizona to spend a week. When the week-end was up, they would ride back to Springfield with me as I would be on my week's leave after Mary Lou's wedding. Louise, Rod and I would bring our trailer back with us to Sierra Vista.

Well, Friday evening finally arrived. Mary and Louise had fried chicken and put together other food for a meal on the way. We took off as soon as Randall was off duty. This turned out to be quite a challenge. Two cars were roaring down the highway. The women were ready for a bite to eat just before Lordsburg, New Mexico. We ate in a short time and decided that Randall would ride with me and Louise and Rod ride with Mary. We could visit as it would be a long night. Randall and I took the lead. It was almost dark. The speed limit in New Mexico at that time was 65 days and 55 night time. There were not any interstates in those days. As soon as we got to the east edge of Lordsburg we were ahead of the women several blocks distance. Randall saw the Port of Entry sign and he said "pull in there. I want to see what restrictions might be in place on pulling trailers on the 4th of July". I was watching for Mary to go by. She did and I knew she did not see us at the Port. I counted three other cars go by. When Randall got back in the car I told him we would have to do a little speeding and pass three cars before we catch the women. They don't know we are behind them now. We added about ten or fifteen mph over the speed limit, passed three cars and caught up with the next one. It was not Mary! We actually could be counted AWOL if we were stopped as we did not have passes. We each had the Fort Huachuca decals on our bumpers to allow us on base.

This chase went on for twenty minutes. We were running about seventy five or eighty. We would pull up behind a car, it would not be the women so I would pass that car and go like the dickens. I got worried that maybe they had pulled off and went back to try to find us as we had no plan on what to do if we got separated. Finally, we caught them! They were running seventy mph trying to catch us. They thought we were ahead and could not figure why we would drive so fast when the night speed limit was fifty-five. We parked my car at an all night filling station with an explanation of being back in two days. We all got in Randall's car. We drove until nine AM Saturday morning, arriving at Randall's parent's house west of Springfield. Uncle Ralph drove down to give Louise, Rod and me a ride to Lamar. I visited family until that evening, then got a ride back to Springfield. I stayed with Randall's parents that night. We left real early pulling the trailer on the 4th of July. It was a good load on his car. Previously he had pulled his trailer with a pickup owned by the company he worked for. We got slowed down on a few hills, but his old Ford managed to always cool off going downhill. It was late in the evening when we reached Alamogordo and got my car. We got to the mountains and it was pitch dark. We stopped as soon as the climb was pulling Randall's car down to a much slower speed. Hooking on with a chain from my car to his, we just went sailing to the top. We unhooked at the top of the mountain and Randall went on down. It was close to midnight when we reached Lordsburg, so we pulled over and we all got a little sleep. We got into Sierra Vista around noon and had the trailer all hooked up to the utilities before dark. I had one more week before my leave was to take effect.

Mrs. Martin and Kenny were ready and we left early on Saturday morning and headed for Colorado. It was just over eight hundred miles to Lamar. We got to Springfield a little after dark and I went on to Lamar, making it there before bedtime.

Mary Lou was married the next day. We got our trailer all loaded with what we needed to take with us. We left the end of the week. We decided to leave in the evening so the temperature would be cooler pulling the trailer at night. Our car did not have air conditioning and it would be easier on the motor to run at night also. When we were in the rolling hills I would speed up to about sixty downhill and would be slowed down usually to about forty going up the upside. Rod was asleep, it was about 10:00 p.m. in New Mexico. Louise said she thought she would sleep for a while. She laid her head in my lap and had fallen asleep. I went down one of those hills going 60 m.p.h. and had just started back up the hill. All of a sudden I saw a full grown steer with long horns standing crosswise on the highway. I swerved to the left to try to miss hitting him. He did not move. I had mirrors on the car that clamped on and stuck out quite a ways. The passenger side mirror hit a horn of the steer. It slammed the mirror on to the side of the car but did not hurt anything. It did, however, wake Louise in a big hurry! After another hour or so she had recovered from this scare and decided to try the sleep mode again. We were doing good time wise. It was midnight when BANG…we blew out a trailer tire. We put the spare on in the dark and once again were traveling. In the early morning we were close to the mountain that I had helped Randall over. It was decided to pull off at a country store and filling station and get some sleep. I knew I could not pull the pass without heating up the old Ford on such a pull. It was not crooked roads, just several miles of steep pulling. We got in the trailer to sleep. It was a hot July day. I managed to fall asleep as I was tired.

About four hours later I woke up to quite a thunderstorm. I told Louise that was good and let's get going and pull the pass in the rain while it was cooler. Just as we started up the pass the sun came out and there went our cooler climb. The car did great. It was close to boiling but we made it with no other trouble. We arrived in Sierra Vista early that evening.

We had a telephone installed in Randall and Mary's trailer with an outside bell on the pole of the line coming in. We had a key to their trailer and if they were gone we could still answer the telephone in case it was a call for us.

Mary got a job at Sears and Roebuck Catalog Store. Louise also got employment there. That helped our income a lot as soldiers pay was not that great. There was an A & W Drive Inn in town where we could get a mug of root beer for a nickel a mug. The baby root beer was free. Rod was having root beer in his baby bottle at age three months!

Homer and Annie tried to sleep in the small building on the lot that was with our trailers. It was not too great an idea as the kitchen and bathroom were in the trailer. They rented a small trailer in a trailer court.

My job driving for Colonel Monohan was great. One time when he and his wife were going out they could not get their regular babysitter. They had me go stay with their children while they went out.

I went to Tucson quite often to pick up personnel flying in for different meetings. Colonel Monohan had a deputy that was just under him. His name was Colonel Adams. His wife lived in Tucson and he went home on week-ends. I often picked him up at his military quarters and drove him to work. His office was in the same building as the General and Colonel Monohan.

There were thirteen different departments under Colonel Monohan in Combat Developments. Sometimes a department head, which was each comprised of a full bird Colonel would leave their area on base and come over to headquarters to talk to Colonel Monohan. They were not furnished drivers or cars. They would use the base taxies like I first drove in the beginning. When they were ready to leave I would take them to their locations on base. This was allowed if I was not busy taking Colonel Monohan or Colonel Adams somewhere. They always liked that as I would uncover the plate on the front of the car that indicated there was an officer on board. This meant that every time we drove past an enlisted man, he would stop and salute. Colonel Adams always told me "just forget to uncover that red plate as I don't want to sit back here and do all that saluting".

Colonel Adams found out that I had never ridden in an airplane. One Friday when I took him to Libby Field on the base, he checked and the L-20 airplane had an extra seat open. He had me ride to Tucson and back. I got to sit in the co-pilot seat, wear the head phones and converse with the pilot. After we were up in the air for a while, the Lieutenant told me he had forgot to shut the phones off that let our talking go out on the air to the base. I guess a lot of people heard my first conversation concerning that first ride. When we landed in Tucson and let everyone off, the pilot suggested we get a coke to drink before heading back to Libby Field. On the ride back, we hit some real rough weather. The pilot could see I was in trouble. He immediately pulled out a bag and handed it to me just in time. I was really sick for a while and stayed that way the rest of the weekend.

Most of my time was the same routine. Sometimes the Mayor of Tucson was here, but I only drove him to the base airport, not to Tucson.

The Secretary of the Army, The Honorable Wilbur Brucker came to visit Fort Huachuca one day. His wife accompanied him. Robbie, General Moorman's driver had the Secretary of the Army, the General and Colonel Monohan in his staff car. I had the General's wife and the Secretary of the Army's wife in my staff car. We drove all over the base and out in the field showing the Army Secretary all around.

Thanksgiving time Louise's parents and her brother Lonnie along with my parents drove to Sierra Vista and spent several days with us. We had Thanksgiving dinner out on our front lawn. Randall and Mary joined us. That Christmas we went to Benson, Arizona and spent the day with Randall's cousin. He had come from the same county in Missouri that my Granddad Clark was from. They introduced us to their friends there who were also from Missouri. This friend remarked that his sister was married to a Keith Clark. It was Carol Keith Clark, whose dad was Abraham Clark, my Dad's first cousin.

This was Rod's first Christmas. Randall's cousins, Bill and Ruth Schriver baby sat Rod while their daughter, Judy, the Martins, and Louise and I went to Tucson to roller skate that Saturday evening.

In February I took leave to go home before being discharged. Randall and Mary rode back to Colorado with us as he had ordered a new Ford Pickup to pull his trailer with. While home on leave, I decided to buy a used pickup to pull my trailer home.

There were two at Baker Motor Company, a 1957 Ford and a 1955 Ford. The '57 was red and white while the '55 was plain green. The '55 was much cheaper so I was thinking if it would work I would buy it and upgrade after I was out of the service. I just did not know if it was as good mechanically as the '57. We went to a valentine's dance on Saturday night. When the dance was over it was snowing hard. Sunday morning we woke up to fifteen inches of snow. That night it was really cold. Monday morning it was close to fifteen degrees below zero. I told Louise and her parents that morning that I was walking the five blocks to the Baker Motor Company to buy one of those pickups. I dressed warm and told the salesman I wanted to hear the '55 Ford run. He said "surely not in this cold weather". I said "yes I do and if it will start I will buy it". It was parked, of course, outside in the cold. I pulled the choke all the way out and it started without any trouble. I knew then that the motor was in pretty good shape, so I bought it. It stayed cold and snowy the rest of the week. We had to use a tractor to pull ourselves in through the pasture at my folks house. We left Lamar to go back to Arizona in sub zero weather. It was good to return to warm weather.

I was discharged in late March on a ninety day early out to return to work as the heavy equipment operator for the ditch company. The man who replaced me while I was in the Army had recently died from infection after having his appendix removed.

The Martins and us went to Tucson where I purchased another tire for the trailer to have a spare. I had not replaced the one that blew out pulling it down to Arizona.

We left for home about mid morning and we were between Lordsburg and Deming, New Mexico when I blew out a tire. It was dark by now. I had a spark plug air pump and was trying to put the tire on the rim when I realized the lock ring for the split rim was not on the wheel. My flashlight was not very bright and I could not locate it in the barrow pit. I decided to take Louise and Rod to the trailer and sleep until daylight and then look for the ring. I was just barely off the road. As soon as a couple of eighteen wheelers went by and the trailer rocked back and forth I changed my mind in a hurry. It was just a two lane road so I could not get away from the traffic much more than I already had. We unhooked and drove on in to Deming at a station that was open yet at midnight. He called a man at a junk yard and I bought a lock ring for the rim. I paid him a good hefty sum for the ring and mounting of the tire. We returned to the trailer, put the wheel on and pulled it where we could get farther off the road. Then we got in the trailer and slept until daybreak. I bought another used tire which I did not have to use and we made it to Lamar around 10:00 a.m. the next day.

Louise's step-grandma Bever had passed away in early February and that house was for sale. With financing help from her Aunt Violet Sneary we bought the house and all the furniture. This was located at 111 North Seventh Street where the family had lived for years. We were both happy to start our lives out together again in the town where we were married nearly two years earlier. I still had to have my hands on a motor or else be tuning an engine. I dug a pit in the old garage and did some motor overhauls and all the tune ups for Jim Labertew's used car business.

My parents would take Rod home with them up at the lakes where they continued to live and Louise's parents would take him to their home to enjoy just three blocks away from us.

My folks still had Clancy, the old '48 Ford pickup I bought before I was drafted. I found an estate sale and bought a pretty nice 1957 Ford custom cab with wrap-around back windows with only fourteen thousand miles on it. It was Inca Gold in color. It was just like new and we used it for travel if we went to Denver or anywhere else. I also used it for my job. We still had our '51 car, so we were very comfortable.

Louise was pregnant with our second child. Rod was now two years old, so our family was growing. While we were taking water down the Amity canal that spring of 1961, I noticed a house with forty acres for sale. It was located in the Goodale community just eight miles west of Bristol. It was a small four room house with a basement, barn and other out buildings including an adobe shop. The owner had lost her husband and wanted a house in Lamar. We were able to trade with the difference in the appraisals paid by us. Louise was not as anxious as I was to move as she had never lived in the country before. Besides it had running water to a kitchen sink but no bathroom, just a path to an outhouse. She knew I wanted it really bad and realized it would be a good place to raise our family. The transaction was completed and we moved Mrs. Looney's household furniture to our house in town and our belongings out there in one weekend. Our parents, Lonnie and Bob Clodfelter helped in the move. He worked for the Amity also. He used the company truck to help us move.

Our new baby was not due until the middle of June. We

hoped to get settled in our new place by then. Louise went into labor on May 25th, four days after our first night living in the country. The baby was stillborn. I named him Dale Lee.

Our new country neighbors were so good to us during this time. We were new to the neighborhood and they all treated us like family, especially the Wilgers and the Smiths.

Jimmie Smith and I were always good friends from my earlier school days at the Goodale School when I was in the second grade. Now we were once again neighbors living only one mile apart. We were both married.

There was much to do at the little farm we purchased. First thing that needed to be done was to put a bathroom in the house. We decided we could use one of the two bedrooms as a bathroom. We bought a used claw footed bathtub and also a used sink and toilet stool. I used the Amity Company's dragline to dig a pit for a septic tank and leach line. Cast iron pipe was used for the drain and sewer line. Back at this time, the heavy plastic pipes were not available. Cast iron had to be cut to length with a chisel and butted against a collar to another piece of pipe. Melted lead was poured into the collar with jute packed in first to keep the hot lead from running out. This took a lot of time and work compared to using PVC pipe today.

While this bathroom was being assembled we used the outhouse and a galvanized round tub for baths. It was quite an adjustment for Louise as she had grown up in town with modern conveniences. I had never had this convenience of an inside tub until I was married. When I was running the bulldozer without any cab on it, the dirt that clung to me was like it was poured on me. One cannot get any dirtier than that! I used an outside garden hose with a sprayer on the end to take the first part of the dirt off. This prompted me to hurry with the installation of the tub and the rest of the bathroom.

We bonded well with all our neighbors, having get-togethers to play cards and 4th of July picnics. Some of the neighbors grew watermelons for seed and did not want us to plant any in our garden as they could cross pollinate and ruin their certified quality. We were told to eat whatever we wanted from their field and enjoy!

The fall of 1961 and less than six months in our country home, the Berlin Crisis had begun overseas. Uncle Sam decided it was time to recall me back into active services. This was not taken very lightly with me. I had served my time in the military. There were others my age group that had not served the first time. It would not only make a hardship on me financially but it would affect my job also as the heavy equipment operator for the Amity Irrigation Company. The person who had filled in for me previously had passed away just prior to my discharge in 1960.

The former Attorney for the Amity had been elected Lt. Governor then became a United States Senator from Colorado. His name was Gordon Allott. He advised me to obtain several letters from businesses in the area and have the Amity Board Members mail them to the Army Reserve for reconsideration of my case and leave me in the Army Reserves and not to activate me.

I was to report to a unit in Lawton, Oklahoma. As the time came closer for me to report for duty, Senator Allott told the Amity Board that it looked like the Reserves was not letting my request be approved. We moved most of our furniture into the basement of the house and the rest into Lamar at the Clark Grandparents house. They had a big house with a lot of room upstairs. I made a topper out of wood for our pickup and loaded in just what we would need to have in an apartment in Oklahoma. Jimmie and Evelyn Smith had to move from their rented farm a mile south of us as it was sold. They bought a farm about two and one half miles east but the house was not fixed up to live in. They were to move in to our place in our absence and give them time to build a house on their newly acquired farm.

The Amity crew and also our Sunday School Class each had a going away party for us. On the last day before leaving with everything either stored on packed up to take with us, I received a telegram that read 'Do Not report for duty to Lawton, Oklahoma'! 'I have contacted the head Army Commander of the Reserves in Omaha, Nebraska and they have placed you back into the Reserves to be left in Colorado'. 'Sincerely, Senator Gordon Allott'.

Well, okay, that meant move everything back home, go back to work and be back to where we were two weeks earlier.

Our first winter in the country, we had a heater oil stove in the living room and a coal/wood stove in the kitchen. There was a round oak coal/wood stove in the basement. The basement had been hand dug under the house by Mr. Looney. We purchased the farm from his widow after he passed away. There was no entrance to the basement except to go outside. We decided to make a laundry chute from the corner of the bathroom to the basement. With a little ladder and a hole for the chute, Rod could go to the basement and up without going outside. We had a bed down there for him to sleep in. We had a little Mexican Collie that slept down there with Rod at night. We thought that would make us feel better knowing that the dog was there with him.

The next spring we obtained a small home improvement loan to build an addition onto our house. I used the Amity dragline and a truck of the Wilger's to dig more basement on the back side of the house that was larger than the original house. We poured cement after the walls were formed. My Dad, Louise's Dad and her brother Lonnie who was now a husky teenager, all helped. We had a pretty good sized cement mixer that belonged to the Amity. I hauled a big load of sand from a sand pit so we only had to buy the cement. This was all done by hand. It took two long days of hard work to make that much cement. I was able to buy lumber for the framing of the upstairs. We had the house closed in before winter. We also had a set of stairs built to go to the basement from inside the house. In November we had our first snow, the same week-end Dwight was born, November 14, 1962. We had gone into Lamar to the Bever Grandparents but Louise did not want to go to the hospital yet. We kept walking around the block. At 11:30 p.m. she finally decided I should get her to the hospital. I was still filling out admission papers when I heard a baby cry. Dwight was born at 11:48 p.m.! Everything went well.

It turned out to be a very cold winter. The Amity Board of Directors decided we should remodel the Amity Office in Holly. All of the ditch riders and maintenance men including me as the Dozer Operator worked on this project. They hired a contractor to oversee the project.

The original office was about twenty-five feet wide and about seventy feet long with fourteen feet ceilings. It was divided into five different rooms. There was a large steel walk-in safe, as it had once been a bank. We gutted the building except for the large safe and the roof. This took away any heat we had but we would sometimes build an open fire in the middle of the building to keep warm. I enjoyed working alongside the other employees who were mostly older than me. This was an experience that taught me some tricks in building our own home.

It stayed so cold that winter that we started having a lot of ice jams in the Kicking Bird Canal, as water was being stored in the Great Plains Reservoirs. This meant that I had to leave the remodeling job and devote most of my time with the ice jams to keep the ice from blocking the canal. Bob Clodfelter, the truck driver and maintenance man, went with me. I needed help to keep my pickup with me. Also, if I had any mechanical problems, Bob was excellent with that type of work. Bob's son, Jim was one year older than me and had gone to High School in Lamar when I did. Jim married Louise's first cousin, Bonnie Sniff and at one time lived next door to her parents when Louise was in high school. They later moved to the Sniff Ranch west of Lamar.

Chapter Eight

My Dad was still working as the Reservoir man to keep tabs on the Lakes and the ditch running the lake water. He was the only one that was not helping with the office remodeling. Mom would do the driving for Dad as his eyesight was very minimal. When we were fighting ice jams at a location called Number Two, there were diversion gates to either send water to the Queen Lakes or else send it to the NeGrande and NeNoshe lakes. This was where most of the ice jams took place. There was an old two room shack located at these gates that had been an old homestead. Dad replaced the windows in this shack and moved Mom's old cook stove there. We could cook chili or whatever in there. We also had an old iron bed with some covers to try to get a little sleep. One time I remember staying up there for eleven days straight and sleeping off and on in that old bed. Most of the time Bob would be with me. If the roads were not snowed shut, Mom and Dad would bring Louise, Rod and baby Dwight along and they would cook a meal in that old stove before going back home that night. Bob used to kid me later and said I was so tired and cold when I got to the shack that I scooted the bed close to the stove that Bob kept burning and would open the oven door and put my feet in there and fall asleep!

The next spring I started looking for my own dragline. I wanted to venture out and be in business for myself. Dad had sold his dry land where the half dugout was located to the State of Colorado Game and Fish Division. He also wanted to buy some land closer to where my family and I lived. He and Mom were also looking for a house in Lamar and retire there.

There was 160 acres in the same section as our 40 acres of irrigated land was. This particular 160 acres was all grassland and also had a good amount of sagebrush and hills on it. It was just what he wanted so he purchased it. They still had not found a house in Lamar and continued to live at the lakes. He did buy a few head of cattle and placed them on the dry land next to us.

In May I was able to buy a used Bantam Dragline. I knew the salesman from the Power Equipment Company in Denver. He thought this one would be just what I needed for starting my own business. It had been used in the Pueblo area and had a back hoe on it. They put a boom on it so I could attach a bucket on it. It was taken to Denver and the boom put on it.

Jimmie Smith, Louise and I took my pickup and drove to the Arvada area to pick it up, or I should say to drive it back home. The bucket they located for me was in a salvage yard and Jim and I struggled to drag that thing close enough so it could be reached with a lift and put into the back of my old Ford pickup. We left Denver the middle of the afternoon. The Bantam was mounted on a F-8 Ford truck. The truck had a full cab on it so I had to let the boom stick out behind me. That meant every time I turned, the boom could wipe someone off the road if I wasn't careful! That was a lot of overhang behind. We finally got out of Denver and made it as far as Limon when it was getting dusk. A patrolman stopped me and told me if I was going to drive after dark then I needed some kind of light on the end of the boom. I said I would stop in Limon and buy some wiring and a red clearance light and let it hang on the end of the boom. He said okay, that would work. I think it was close to 11:00 p.m. that night when we made it home. That was one long day!

My first job was to dig a slush pit for Jirld Wilger where they were going to drill an irrigation well.

My second job was over a hundred hours of work. Ray Gilbert, who owned land next to Dad up at the lakes, had always wanted to develop an irrigation project by digging a canal in a very seepage area next to the dry land lake bottom. Mr. Gilbert had told me for several months that I needed to buy a dragline so I could dig this ditch to develop a water system to be able to pump water to a field that could be planted to alfalfa.

This was 1963 and I purchased a John Deere B with a mount-on lister. I was farming my place with it. When I was not running the dragline, I was farming. As fall was approaching and being new in running my own business, I needed any work I could get. Most of what I was doing was small jobs with the exception of Mr. Gilbert's water exploration.

There were two other businesses in the Lamar area doing earth moving. Both had draglines, dozers and dump trucks. They were in competition with each other and each did not want to let the other to have any job they could get. This was a plus for me as I got along with each of them and had even been offered a partnership position with one of them. This happened while I was still employed by the Amity. We never closed the transaction but still continued our friendship.

One of the contractors called me to say he had a job up by Eads and Kit Carson that he would not be able to do for a while and asked if I was interested. It involved unloading several railroad cars of a base rock to be used by C.I.G., a gas company for their big compressor site. The problem was that I did not have a clam shell to reach into the railroad cars and put the rock on the ground. I told the contractor that I would like the job but I did not have a clam shell to put on my dragline. He said 'no problem, I have one and will let you use it'. This job was not as easy as it sounded because I could not see over into the railroad car to tell exactly where the rock was. I managed to get the job done.

This was located right beside the highway so I was very noticeable while working here. A gentleman who lived in Kit Carson and owned a large ranch west of where I was working stopped and introduced himself to me. He needed some ponds dug on a creek that ran through his ranch for his cattle to have an abundant supply of water. I told him I would be glad to do the job. His newly married grandson, Charles Weber, lived on the ranch and was taking care of the cattle. I ate dinner with Charles and his wife every day I worked there. Janelle was a good cook so there was lots of fried chicken, etc. They were exceptionally nice people and it sure beat eating out of my lunch pail. I am still friends with Charles as he later became a brand inspector as did one of their sons years later and lives in Lamar at this time.

After completing this job, several ranchers north of Kit Carson also had ponds that were fed with live water, but needed the mud cleaned out. The mud was holding back the water. I kept going from ranch to ranch for quite a few ranchers. They did not have anyone doing this type of work closer to them. The problem was that I was driving eighty or ninety miles one way each day but I needed the work. It was getting late into fall and I knew I needed to work closer to home, so I finally said I would come back the next summer and do more pond cleaning if I had time.

When I was employed by the Amity much of my work was in the Holly area. I knew most of the farmers in the area. There had been a construction company that had been doing dragline work in that area but had moved out of state, There was work in this area for me, which was closer to home.

The Buffalo Canal, which is a smaller canal, needed some work done but had no equipment of their own to do the work. Their ditch rider and acting superintendent had operated a bulldozer for Wilson Construction until they moved out of state. Bill Glover and I had worked side by side many times after a big rain, with washouts on the Amity Canal and the Kickingbird Canal and also when they needed extra equipment to help repair the breaks caused by floods. Bill was old enough to be my dad but we had great respect for each other and were good friends. Bill arranged for me to do the work on the Buffalo Canal with my dragline. In return, I gave them a break on the hourly charge if they would let me do their maintenance when I was not busy with other jobs. I also gave them priority on any emergency work they needed done. This guaranteed me steady work. The Amity also called on me when they needed extra work.

I bought a small bulldozer in early 1964 that was a great help along with the dragline. I also acquired a truck to haul the dozer and use for hauling dirt and gravel if needed.

Another canal just inside the Kansas border east of Holly was only a distance of about ten miles long. This was the Frontier Ditch and they hired me to do their heavy equipment work also. I stayed busy with ditch digging jobs, tree removal, farming and building onto our home.

Louise's parents and my parents became close friends. They played cards together often and shared events with their grandchildren. They would come to the country to our home often.

When my parents were still living at the lakes, we spent a lot of Sundays at their house. One time when we were at their place, Rod and Dwight were outside playing. Rod was around five years old and Dwight was not quite two years old. When Louise and I went outside to check on them, Rod was visible but we could not find Dwight. The lake was not very far from the house. We called and called but no answer. I headed for the lake but he still was nowhere to be found. The grandparents were worried as was Louise. I was too, but was certain he was just not where we could see him or answer back. Finally, I looked in the back of a Chevy Coupe that had belonged to my Uncle Fred. I had taken the motor out to put in a Chevy pickup I had bought. Dwight had crawled into that car with no back seat and had crawled into the trunk and was sound asleep. The scare and hunt was over.

On May 21, 1965 Tim was born in Lamar. The day I went to town just before noon to bring Louise and baby Tim home, Dr. Krausnick met me in the hallway. He said 'Keith that boy of yours has a problem and I want you to take him straight from here to Children's Hospital in Denver'. He said he could experiment with some things, but that would just drag him down if he did not find the problem. 'They have specialists in Denver and let's get him where they know what is going on'. He said he was not holding food down and will get weaker and weaker if he doesn't eat.

Louise borrowed a dress from her mother. I had a white t-shirt on. We filled the car with gas and we took off to Denver. Between Limon and Denver we encountered a real severe thunderstorm with lots of hail. When we arrived at Children's Hospital we needed coats as it was very cold. We entered Tim in the hospital and spent the night with relatives. They told us they were running tests on Tim and that we probably should go back home while they were doing them. Tim was so healthy looking and was the biggest of the three boys. We couldn't comprehend the possibility that there could be something wrong with him. We hated to leave him but we each needed clothes and decided to go home. I think it was on Saturday morning. We got home and checked with the grandparents and Rod and Dwight. Early the next morning we called the hospital to check on our baby son. The nurse, who took my call checked on him, came back to the telephone and told me that he was not breathing right and if I wanted to see him we had better get back to Denver.

It did not take us long before we were in the car and this was probably one time when I added some miles per hour on to the speed limit. We were so scared!

When we walked into the hospital we asked the nurse at the nurse's station how our baby was. She looked at us and said 'you can take him home, we know what his problem is and he is going to be fine'. We were so glad he was going to be alright that we did not investigate how a nurse got the wrong file or whatever the mix-up was about him earlier that gave us false information.

It turned out the muscles at the bottom of his esophagus had spasms and would not keep any nourishment down. He needed to be fed with his upper torso at an angle and we gave him special milk at that time called Similac.

In June 1965 it started raining really hard for several days. We had about twelve inches at our place and south and west of Lamar it rained as much as twenty one to twenty five inches in one night! This caused the creeks, canals and the Arkansas River to flood. The dam west of Lamar stopped the water at that point, but all the creeks below the dam flooded the river as well as the creeks south and east of Lamar. These were the Granada Creek, Clay Creek, Cat Creek, Mud Creek and Butte Creek. This flood had water in houses in Lamar, Granada, Holly and on into Kansas at Coolidge, Syracuse and on east. Louise's parent's house had about eighteen inches inside and the cellar full. My folks lived far enough south of the river that they didn't have any water in their house.

Our home site was far enough north of the river that we only had to worry about the Amity Canal which runs through our place about two hundred feet from our house. We were afraid the canal would break. We were fortunate that it did not break.

Just before the flood, I had been getting ready to do a job in the river bottom land right north of Granada with the dragline. I had just completed a job with the bulldozer directly north of Granada and had moved the bulldozer to the home of Bruce Rader on the hillside closer to Bristol. The water in Granada and also north of Granada where I had the bulldozer earlier in the week had water about six feet deep. The only reason I had both pieces of my equipment at this spot was that I was in the process of changing the dragline motor over to propane and needed a part to complete the change.

I was fortunate to live where I was safe from flooding. My neighbor to the north, Leabert Brazell and I were able to get to Eads and go to the grocery store. We had moved in with them for a few days as we were without electricity. We moved a propane cook stove into their house to cook on. We needed groceries and Tim's special milk. On the way back home from Eads we saw the State of Colorado Highway Department officials talking. We stopped to talk to them. The head of the highway department, Dale Cross was there. He was originally from Lamar but working out of Pueblo now.

Tim wanted to be just like dad after Keith had eye surgery in 1967

Mr. Cross was a special friend to my Dad, Uncle Ralph and my Grandpa Clark. His wife was raised down south of Lamar close to Clay Creek Store that my Dad and Granddad once owned. I had gone to high school with Melvin and Ilene, son and daughter of Mr. Cross.

Mr. Cross asked me where my equipment was. I told him where my dragline and bulldozer was located. They were located less than a fourth mile from the first washed out bridge on Highway 385 between Granada and Bristol. Mr. Cross said that he would like to hire me to work for the State of Colorado using my equipment. He said he had two twenty- cubic- yard Ukes to be there first thing the next morning and they can start hauling fill dirt to the washed out bridges and tubes across the highway. I told him I would be there first thing in the morning. We worked two full days and just before dark the second day we made the washout passable. There were lots of people walking from Granada to Bristol to help one another. The power line poles were laid down flat but the wires were not broken. People were trying to pick up the poles with other timber to get the lines off the ground so electricity could be restored. I took the dragline and the men would tie the bucket of the dragline onto the pole high enough up that I could stand the poles back up so they could prop them up. We did this all the way to Granada while there was still enough light to work.

The next morning I drove to Granada. There were residents throwing stuff out of their flooded homes. Yards were full of trash, flooded cars, junk and all sorts of things. My dozer was only a fourth mile out of town where I had been using it. I drove the dozer to Uncle Arley's house, who was Louise's Dad's brother, where I dozed out his back yard including any yard fence that was left. It was so sad to see all of this, especially for Uncle Arley and Aunt Armold.

I worked most of July and part of August around Granada, Lamar and Holly on highways 50 and 385 for the State of Colorado. They paid very well. They paid a fee as rental for each piece of equipment and also paid me operator wages. I had hired an operator for the bulldozer to help me as I could only run one machine at a time.

By the end of August it was also time to fulfill my obligation to the Buffalo Canal doing repair work after the land dried out.

Everything seemed to happen at once. I had applied for a

postal position with the Lamar Post Office several years earlier and received a letter stating there was an opening at the Post Office. I was to schedule the exam. I did not know what to do, but decided that this was an opportunity that would only happen once. What the heck as it would only be a part time position.

I took the exam knowing that with my military time I would automatically receive an extra five points as I was a veteran. I passed the test and was number three on the list. There must have been over fifty that had taken the exam also. The Postmaster called me in for an interview and told me he could hire any of the top three but he notified five of us in case any of the top three decided not to accept the position. I had a high enough score that the Postmaster asked me to come to work. So here I am still busy with my heavy equipment, but my main hours at the Post Office would be from 6:00 a.m. to 9:30 a.m. and then 4:00 p.m. to 6:00 p.m. and work every other Sunday. I could run the dragline in between the time schedule and farm and take care of the cattle in the evening. I was soon putting in sixty hours some weeks as I did not receive overtime. They used the part time employees more than the regulars.

I hired an experienced dragline operator and concentrated on doing just dozer work. I soon was filling in on carrier routes as there were four of us part time employees, two used as clerks and two used as carriers. The three carrier routes each only worked forty hours. I was filling in on all three routes. One of the regular carriers had an alcohol problem so I was always subbing on his route. I continued this pace until this particular carrier resigned. I then became a regular with days off during the week. This was five years after I first started as a substitute.

The Clark Family in December 1966

Chapter Nine

We wanted to add a daughter to our family so we put in for adoption. This was in 1969. We had filled out all the proper papers and were told we were on the waiting list for a daughter. Almost a year had gone by with no word from the State of Colorado. We checked with Social Services and found out our file had been 'misplaced'!

Finally the end of January of 1970 we received a telephone call that a baby girl was available in Littleton, Colorado. It was February 4th when we drove to Littleton. The baby girl had been born on September 19, 1969. They brought her out into the room where we had been told to stay and left her with us for a while. They then asked if we wanted to proceed with the possibility of adopting this baby.

She was a beautiful four and a half month old baby with red hair. We were overjoyed! She was released to us and we drove to my brother, Lonnie's home in Denver. He and his wife, Candy, had a daughter born just one month before Pam's birth, on August 19, 1969. We named our daughter Pamela Lynn. After introducing the two little cousins, we headed back home. Pam did not even let out a whimper all the way home until we were entering Prowers County rounding the curve on Highway 287 south of Eads. She really cut loose and cried then! I guess she figured why not let us know she did have a set of lungs after all. It was too far to take her back!

When we arrived in Lamar Rod, Dwight and Tim were at

their Bever grandparents home. The Clark grandparents were there also. They all wanted to get a firsthand look at this new sister and granddaughter. It was about eight o'clock in the evening.

Back to my new position at the Post Office, my route was a walking route, which I enjoyed. It was hot in the summer and cold in the winter but it was nice in between those seasons and the undesirable days weren't that bad. My route was the most established one in town with the patrons having been there the longest. Some of the joys on my route were to be able to deliver mail to my parents, my Grandma Clark, two former teachers, Mrs. Brase and Mrs. Guy, the parents of Senator Allott's wife and many of my classmates parents.

When some of my more elderly patrons could not get out to their mailbox very well I would rap on their door and set their mail just inside for them. This, of course, was not in the rules of the Post Office delivery, but it did not take any extra time as just a few faster steps would keep me on time. After a lot of these elderly people moved into the nursing home, I made it a practice to go visit them on Sunday afternoons. A lot of them had no relatives in the area to go visit them. One lady in particular was past 100 years old and still lived in her small house. She had a good mind and was always neat and well dressed. When she moved to the nursing home at age 102 I would visit with her there. I would take Louise and also Pam, who was now a preschooler with me. She so much enjoyed our little red headed Pam as not many children were visitors in the nursing home unless they were visiting a close relative.

Once I thought that a three wheeled tricycle would work and

Pamela Lynn Clark's first picture.

I could carry the mail easier. I rented a three wheeled tricycle. It had a drawback. I had to pull my mail out of the case different in order to go straight up a street and down. When I walked, I would zigzag several times back and forth across each block. It could have worked okay if I had made my letter case at the Post Office permanent to this route design, but what would happen when I had twelve inches of snow to go through? I would have to walk again and would have to line up my mail sequence over again.

I had two houses on my route where blind people lived. The single man would take his white cane and could go seven or eight blocks to the grocery store or the post office where he would ride with a star route carrier with his truck load of mail to Springfield, Colorado, fifty miles south or on to Walsh, another twenty five miles. Mr. Haney was a piano tuner.

One time Mr. Haney was by the rock wall at the football stadium and was going first one way, then another. I knew he was in trouble. I asked if he was having a problem. He said he could not figure out where he was. I told him where he was and also which direction he was facing. He thanked me and I watched for a little while and he was okay.

The other couple, Ralph and Laura Hunter, never walked away from their home. Ralph would water his lawn by feeling his way around his yard and knew from the location of the sidewalk where he was. Mr. Strong always picked up the Hunters and Mr. Haney to take them to Church. They attended the Christian Church.

At times some of my patrons mail boxes came off the stands or broke. One person had their mailbox mounted on the top of a very large chain with links about six inches around. They had been welded together and one of the welds broke. He asked who he should get to weld the broken link. I told him when I got off work that evening I would weld it for him. I loved welding and I also enjoyed the opportunity to help out one of my patrons. I also had a number of experiences doing some minor work on vehicles. Usually it was an old Ford that I had quite a few spare parts for anyway. One day an elderly lady had a 1964 Ford and she was waiting for me to drive up in my mail jeep with her mail. She told me she was just 'sick' as her Ford would not shift into high gear on the automatic transmission. At that time I had a 1965 Mercury similar to her Ford. I had the same problem and I had a vacuum hose come unhooked. I very quickly said I would look under her hood and sure enough, the hose was off. She told me that a service station told her they could replace the transmission but it would cost around one thousand dollars. I hooked the hose back on for her. The next day she was waiting for me once again to deliver her mail. She gave me a big box of chocolates for fixing her car! These last few stories were after my route became a mounted route with a jeep. Some of the mailboxes were at the curb.

The years that I was still a substitute carrier, on Christmas Day all of the substitutes would come in as soon as he mail truck from Pueblo arrived at 6:00 a.m. We would sort all of the first class letters and box them in the post office boxes. We also sorted the packages and delivered the city packages to residents. We could usually do this in short day and be through by 11:00 a.m. and be home for Christmas Dinner. One sub would return in the evening to tie out the incoming letters dropped in the Post

Office and placed into mail sacks and send out with the truck to Pueblo.

When people used to order baby chickens or geese, etc. they were shipped by the mail system. We would call the person who ordered them as soon as they came into the Lamar Post Office so they could be picked up. Robert Wheeler, who owned and operated a truck that took the mail south to the smaller towns, delivered the chickens, etc. with him. A pickup with a topper owned by another contractor took the mail to Granada, Bristol, Hartman and Holly. Wiley and McClave had another contractor for those towns. Occasionally honey bees and a shipment of lady bugs were also shipped into the Post Office for area farmers.

In 1966 we purchased a small overhead camper. It was not big but had the basics such as ice box, stove, sink and water tank, but no toilet. We loved going to the mountains. We also took it to Wyoming and Missouri. We purchased a boot to go between the pickup cab and camper by taking the rear pickup window and the front camper window out and the boot was placed between the two and aired up to make a seal between them. This allowed the boys and those in the front seat to talk to each other. We even took Dad and Mom Clark with us to Missouri on one trip. They would spend nights at various cousins while my family and I stayed in the camper. We had an overhead bed that the three boys slept in and the table folded down for a bed for Louise and me. It was a tight fit for the boys but it worked and we had fun! The three boys soon had outgrown the overhead bed.

Soon after Pam was added to our family we realized the pickup camper was just too small for all of us. We didn't think we could afford a larger camper and we would need a larger pickup if we went that route. We thought we could find an old school bus and convert it into a camper. One of my neighbors, Jim Rogers had an older Chevy Bus, about a 1946 model. All but the driver's seat had been removed. It had a bed in the back that his brother used when he was down to help with the farming. Jim indicated he would like to have my pickup camper, so we swapped. I got a couple hundred dollars in the deal so I could use it to get camper equipment.

When summer got here we wanted to go to the mountains in the bus. We went to Westcliff to a campground. We had not done much to the inside of the bus. We put in sleeping bags, had the old bed in the back and we took water jugs and food in ice chests. The old bus was noisy, pretty slow and needed lots of loving care. Later that year, one of my classmates, Jerry Smith, and I were visiting and he told me someone had wrecked a pickup with a very large camper and he bought it and removed all of the interior from it. He had thought about building another camper but said he would sell me all the equipment if we could come to an agreement on a price. We made a deal. I got a two compartment stainless steel sink, a thirty gallon water tank and gauge, a hot water heater that was a ten burner propane instamatic heater, a refrigerator that was electric or propane, a three burner cook stove and a bathroom stool and holding tank. All of this equipment had not been damaged in the wreck.

About the same time that I bought this camper equipment I found out that the Prowers County 4-H had purchased a school bus and had it serviced but somehow the oil plug had not been put in tight. The oil ran out of the motor on one of their first trips. A new rebuilt motor had been installed, but the 4-H Council decided not to use the bus again for transporting the members. It was put up for sale. It was a 1951 Ford with a V-8 engine. The body and other mechanical parts were in good shape so we purchased it.

Our neighbor, Jim Smith wanted the other old bus to remove the body and make a farmhand out of the frame and motor.

We removed most of the seats from this newer bus and built a closet, bathroom walls and two three quarter sized bunk beds on one side. We put in the dinette table that was part of the wrecked camper and had a pedestal that I mounted on the floor. The table top could be removed and placed between the seats for a bed. We took our time fixing it up. We painted all the inside, Louise made curtains and the plywood was a good grade wood that we used for the inside. We also had a propane light mounted on the wall in the dinette area as well as the twelve volt lights. Oh yes, as Pam was under two years old at this time, her bed was a large dresser drawer that we could store under a bus seat that was part of the dinette area!

I installed a forty gallon propane tank on the frame as well as a thirty gallon extra gas tank. We bought a large Servelle Refrigerator that ran on propane from a friend. This was much larger than the regular camper refrigerator. A large freezer on top held a large amount of food and was excellent for long stays away from home. We raised our own beef so had plenty of room to take some with us.

We worked many nights and days to get this 'motor home' ready by Labor Day. The 1951 model of course was six volt so I mounted a second generator on it that was twelve volt. This way if we ran the lights, water pump and twelve volt things until we run the battery low, it did not matter as I still had the original six volt battery that ran the bus. I had a very large twelve volt John Deere battery installed for the camper accessories. We took the bus to San Isabel and had a great time. Les and Betty Scriven and their children, David and Melinda often went with us on camping trips even in the pickup camper, or borrowing her uncle's camper or just pitching a tent. We enjoyed our outings with these special friends.

We started talking about taking a big trip the next summer. We wanted to go to a cousin reunion with the Gaydons. Two of the older sisters still lived in Star Valley Wyoming, right below Jackson Hole. It was planned for the summer of 1972. We took Dad and Mom Clark with us in the bus. We met up with Ted and Vonnie and their children, David, Terri and Julie in Green River, Wyoming. We did not have a tow vehicle to take behind the bus but it was in A-1 shape so I was confident it would work out okay. Ted and his family had a fold up camper he pulled with his car. We spent the night close to an area called LaBarge Road. This was a road that went through mountain country. We had been through there several times in our pickup camper. It is very remote and was a logging and lumber road, but very beautiful back woods country. The next morning when we took off on this shortcut that would take us out to a main road into the south part of Star Valley, we could see there was more and more snow along the road. One place we had to pull out off the road to the side to get around a big snow drift. Pretty soon the road had about six feet of snow for a long way and had not been opened up at all. We had to turn around and go back out! We had a little trouble getting the bus turned around in the narrow road. After lots of back and forth moving we finally got turned back. We unhooked Ted's camper from his car and turned it around by hand. Then he had no problem getting his car turned around. About this time there was a moose within fifty yards of the snow that made us stop. He was huge and stood there and looked at us for a while before retreating back into the trees. We backtracked on the trail to the highway towards Big Piney. We went on north to Hoback Junction, just below Jackson Hole then joined up to the north end of Star Valley and on to Elmer and Rayma Wolfley's home in Etna, Wyoming. After a day or so at their place the rest of the cousins arrived. We all traveled north just below the Teton Mountains. We were the only group in this area. We hiked on into the back country, went fishing and told lots of stories! We all went back to the Wolfley place. Some of the families went on to their homes. After our several more days at their home, my family and Ted and family went on up to Yellowstone National Park for several days. Dad and Mom stayed with Rayma and family. When we pulled the bus away from our camp site in the Park, Ted parked his car in that spot to save it. Their family of five and our family of six boarded our bus and toured all around the park. At night we would return to the campground and be ready to go again the next morning. We have wonderful memories of that trip!

Our bus averaged ten miles to the gallon of gas and gas was cheap, so it was a lot of trip for the money! We picked up Dad and Mom and headed back to Colorado.

In the fall of 1972 I wanted to buy a small Datsun pickup to drive to work to the Post Office. I wanted to make a tow bar and tow it behind the bus. It could be used for transportation, sight seeing and getting into places the big bus could not go. At this particular time everyone was wanting a small pickup, but not many were available to purchase. We traveled to Pueblo and tried out a Datsun, a Toyota, a Courier and a Chevy Luv. None was available. I had to get on a waiting list. A couple of weeks went by and the Datsun dealer called me that they had several Datsuns come in. As soon as I had a day off from the Post Office we went to Pueblo, but by this time they were all sold. The Chevy dealer had a Chevy Luv. We bought it. It was not my choice for a small pickup but it would have to do. It only had room for one child besides Louise and I so we purchased a nice topper cover where the boys could ride in the back. It averaged around twenty-four m.p.g. so was very economical.

In 1974 we planned a trip to Disney World. The Post Office did not usually let anyone take time off at Christmas time, but had approved a two week leave for me. I did not start my leave until Christmas Day. One of my co-workers, Wade Heinsen, had bought a fold up trailer that was quite large with an ice box, stove and lots of bed space. He wanted to store it in my shop for the winter and said I could use it to take to Florida. I had a new forty foot by forty foot shop that Louise and I built the summer of 1972 so I had plenty of room to store his camping trailer.

This was a trip that we often talk about. We had a great time the two weeks we were gone. The teachers approved taking the children out of school for a week. They said they would learn more from the trip than if they were in school!

We drove to Dumas, TX and spent Christmas night with Leabert and Billie Brazell. We went to church that evening with them. The next day we went just east of Dallas and spent the night at a campground. The next day we were at Vicksburg, Mississippi. We wanted to tour the Civil War Battleground. The next day we woke up to a steady rain, so it spoiled our getting out of the car to visit the memorials. Instead we drove through the battleground. The following day we arrived in Slidell, Louisiana, right next to New Orleans. We camped on the gulf at a campground that had sea shells for gravel on the roads and campsites. We took a boat ride that went through coves and bayous where the Mississippi River dumped into the gulf. We traveled through Biloxi and on into Panama City, Florida. There we ate our first delicious shrimp dinner. We also visited a former minister who had served at the First Christian Church in Lamar, Phillip Durham and his wife.

We traveled on down the coast of Florida, crossed over to the Atlantic Ocean side and got into a campground close to Disney World. We were camping right in the middle of an orange grove and the aroma was wonderful.

We went to Cape Kennedy, Sea World, Daytona Beach Race Track and Disney World. We were in Disney World on New Year's Day, 1975. We visited the Hall of Presidents that were wax figures and automated to stand up and talk. At five years old, we could not convince our daughter, Pamela, that they were not real people!

We followed the coast on up to Georgia and on into Florence, South Carolina where we visited my cousin and her family, Don and Pat Weeks. Pat was the oldest child of the Angell cousins. She taught school there. She was also the oldest of the Clark grandchildren. We spent several days with them. Pat drove us all around the area of Florence. Don was an entomologist

The Clark Family taken in 1974

and worked for the State of South Carolina and was very knowledgeable of the area, knew about every tree and vine there was around there. It was a very educational visit.

We headed on to Tennessee and it was a lot colder there. We stayed at Crossville in a campground. The trailer was uncomfortable because of the weather. After setting up the camper, we drove downtown to a grocery store. There were cured hams hanging on hooks from the ceiling and a lot of other grocery items we never had in Colorado. The next day we were in Knoxville but we just drove through Opryland as our time was running short on our vacation. We stayed in Little Rock, Arkansas where once again there was a steady rain. When we cranked up the camper for the night there was a bang sound on the gears while cranking. When we were ready to fold it up the next morning, it would not lower on one end.

I finally bought an assortment of screwdrivers and found one that would fit into the screws on the inside of the camper wall. When I removed enough screws to look inside the unit, I could see that the cable had snapped and was all wound up in there. By the time I finally got it unwound, and the camper shut, I was soaked from working in the rain all morning.

Our next stop was Shattuck, Oklahoma to visit Randall and Mary Martin and family. We decided not to set up the camper that evening. I could still get into the camper thru the half door to get clothes. We spent the night in a warm house with them.

After a few days at home, I took the camper apart again at the place where the cable was tangled. It needed a metal part that I was able to purchase and got it fixed.

Wade decided he did not want to keep the camper and sold it to another Postal employee. We decided we would never be happy with any camper with canvas walls and ceiling. When the beds on each end were pulled out the condensation formed on the ceiling above the beds. The high humidity in Florida did not help. We had to use bath towels each morning to wipe down the canvas ceiling from the beds before we could fold it up again.

In the summer of 1975 we had a colt that I raised. He was half Arabian and half quarter horse. He was green broke. Dwight wanted to ride him. Dwight was twelve years old at this time. I got home from work and was running irrigating water. I remember telling Dwight that I would saddle up the horse, set the irrigation water, and ride him first before letting him ride. Then next thing I remember is waking up in a bed with three or four men from the Church, including Barrett McCanless, Dick Bolinger, and Louise standing beside me. I hurt from one end to the other and I remember asking Louise what in the world happened, was I in a car wreck? She said 'no, you were in a horse wreck!' I answered her by saying 'my gosh, a person could wake up dead!'

To this day, I do not remember anything from setting water to the hospital room. I was told I got on the horse and Dwight said I rode him out onto the gravel county road in front of the house, a car went by and the horse reared up and fell over backwards with me on him. The horse scrambled, kicked me in the head and got up. The saddle was an old one that had belonged to my Uncle Cliff. It did not have a covered saddle horn. The saddle horn penetrated me in the groin just missing my main artery and ripped me for about six inches. Louise had looked out the window and ran out to the road. She said I asked her to get me out of the road before someone ran over me. Our neighbor boy, Jim Wilger was going home on his motorcycle. He jumped off his motorcycle and drove us in our 1971 Ford to the hospital. The car had a powerful 429 motor in it. When he got to 100 mph Louise said she was scared but also scared of speed, so he slowed down a bit. Anyhow, that is the story I was told.

Chapter Ten

I spent a week in the hospital before being released to go home. While in the hospital one evening I looked up and in walked Rod with his friend, Glen Shefferd with a brown paper sack with something fairly large in it. I thought maybe it was a milkshake but when Rod got over to the bed he pulled out a starter that had been on his 1964 Ford. He was starting to tinker with cars like I had always done. He wanted to ask me a question about it, so he brought it in for me to look at.

I want to give credit to my Lord and Saviour, Jesus Christ, for looking after me once more. My Jesus truly cares about me and keeps His loving arms around me.

After Christmas in 1976 we were invited to go to a square dance in Tribune, Kansas. We started attending their monthly dances. I had never had lessons, but Louise had been in Dudes and Dames when she was younger. The people were really helpful to us and we value the friendships we made there. Lessons were being given in Syracuse, Kansas for beginner square dancers and we signed up to take the lessons. We felt more comfortable after taking lessons and were soon traveling around the area on Saturday night. Dances were held in Tribune, Syracuse and Johnson, Kansas on different Saturday nights. We made many friends in these towns in the late 1970's. Our children would go with us and go to the theatre in Tribune and Syracuse. I would pick them up after the movie and take them back to the dance just as it was ending. Lots of time it would be midnight when we would get home, but we always got up and attended Sunday School and Church. There was never alcohol allowed at the square dances.

In June on a Saturday afternoon in 1977 I hurried home from working at the Post Office as there was a big square dance with a special caller we wanted to attend. We had rented a rug shampooer to use on our carpet. It was a very hot day and I very hurriedly shampooed the carpet and went to the basement to shower and cool off. I had not been in the shower but just for a minute or two when it felt like something hit me in the back of the head. Things were whirling so I just stepped out of the shower and lay down on the floor. My head was hurting and I felt sick but I thought that was stupid of me to cool off so quickly after being hot and sweaty from hurrying around. I got up off the floor, dried off and went upstairs. Louise looked at me and asked if I was all right. I said I cooled off too fast but I'll soon be o.k. We left for the square dance being held in Syracuse. I danced about one tip, but was sicker than I was at home and my head was throbbing. Louise had been having a lot of back trouble and going to a chiropractor in Syracuse for treatments. Dr. Butts had been the one that encouraged Louise to square dance to help her back. He and his wife were square dancers and at the dance that evening. He asked me what was wrong and I told him what had happened in the shower. He suggested a treatment on my neck and head would help so we went to his office downtown. I was still in much pain that I thought we should go home. Sunday morning it felt like my eyes were going to blow out of my head. I tried pain relievers but nothing helped. I went to several Doctors in Lamar seeking help. Finally, one of them sent me to Denver to Porter Hospital. My blood pressure was really high. I remember the Doctor said it was 120 over 110. I asked him what happens when they meet. He looked at me and said 'you're dead'! After many test they finally took me to Swedish Hospital for a cat scan, the only place available to get one at that time. It did not show anything unusual. My headache was easing up after nearly a week and I wanted to go home. The Doctor said he would release me but wanted to do one more test. He pulled spinal fluid from my spine and it showed blood in it. They really got excited then and wouldn't let me out of bed or even sit up. I was told I had had a hemorrhage. They transferred me back over to Swedish Hospital in an ambulance and directly into intensive care for the rest of the weekend. I was put in a room the first of the week and the testing started. I was asked if I would share a room with a smoker but I declined.

At this point in my story I want to dwell on my roommate. The room I was moved to was occupied by a young man at least ten years younger than me. There was a young woman and several other people standing beside his bed talking to him. They introduced themselves to me. My roommate was Peter Gcrrald. The others were his wife, his mother, his minister and a gentleman handling some legal documents for them. It turned out they were doing a will for Peter. When they finished the necessary work with the papers they needed signatures from several people, including witnesses to sign the paperwork. They asked if I would be willing to be a witness. I willingly agreed. At that time I thought to myself that this guy, Peter, looks healthy and I wish I was that healthy at the moment.

After the room was cleared of visitors and just Peter and I to talk, he told me he had an operation a year earlier for a tumor in his lower neck that had returned and was cancerous. He told me he was not worried because he had Jesus and was only worried about those people who were not Christians. He said his faith was Free Methodist and he was employed as a chemist for the U. S. Geological portion of the government. After a few hours of being alone with each other, I could see we were destined to be roommates. He lived in the south area of Denver close to the Swedish Hospital.

I told him I had lived in the southeastern corner of Colorado all my life. He asked me if I knew where Camp Amache was, close to the town of Granada. This was really a surprise as I told him I lived about eleven miles as he crow flies from Camp Amache and I could stand in front of my home and see the trees across the Arkansas River that had been planted there by the Japanese during their interment there. He said his father was a guard here during the Second World War.

He stated he had always wanted to visit there where his father had been a guard. We soon got to know a lot about each other and our respective families as we spent three weeks together in the same room. He had a daughter and two sons all under ten years of age.

While I was there those three weeks I had a lot of relatives and friends come to visit me. Our good friends, the Scrivens' brought up my sons and daughter to visit me. Rev. Schweissing, former pastor of the First Baptist Church in Lamar came to visit. I was good friends with his oldest son in high school.

One of my tests was an angiogram on my brain and said I

had an artery in the back of my head that had leaked, but could not pinpoint the exact spot to repair it. I had to wait another two weeks before they could repeat the test.

This let Peter and I do lots of talking as neither of us could get out of bed. I was to stay in bed until the next angiogram so that I would not put any extra pressure on the artery. After two weeks another angiogram was performed and still could not pinpoint where the spot on the vessel was. They let me go home for two weeks and I was not to lift over five pounds or drive and then return for yet another angiogram.

When we returned to Denver we took some packages of our home raised beef for Peter and Carol and family. He had been told there was nothing further that could be done for him and was sent home.

This time at the hospital I was all hooked up with tubes and was connected to the screen and monitor and the Doctors became very excited. They then discovered there was another Steven Clark with the same condition. They had pulled the wrong chart! Thank goodness they figured that one out. After the test I was told I had scar tissue over the artery and to the best of their knowledge it was healed but wanted to see me in a year for a repeat test. I believe in the power of prayer and I know the One who healed me, my Jesus.

When I returned home and back to work I soon found out from my mail patrons that every church in town had me on their prayer list.

I was to see a neurologist that came down to Lamar once a month. This Doctor was a great person. When he came to Lamar he wore a big western hat and cowboy boots! We always had a good time just chatting. I was always his last client of the day when I got off work. I decided to play a little joke on him one time. Doctors use these special tools that are kind of like stainless steel spoons. It would be put on your cheek and ask if it felt hot or cold. He also had this small hammer to tap your knee to see how your reflex was. I decided if I really concentrated when he tapped on one knee, I would kick my other knee up! He suddenly looked up at me with a puzzled look then began to laugh. I did, too!

When I returned to work at the Post Office in was late summer of 1977. Rod, Dwight and Tim were old enough to look after things at home and in the pasture.

Several months later in the fall I received a telephone call early one morning. It was Carol Gerrald on the other end of the line. She said, "Keith, Peter in on his last few hours we think. He cannot hold the telephone but he wants to talk to you". He said "I can still tell people I have Jesus with me and I will be all right. I can still witness to others". Later that day Carol called back and told me Peter had passed away.

Carol did come down a few months later, bringing her children with her for a visit. I have never known another person as strong in their faith as Peter was. He made a big impact on my life.

When I was a 4-H Leader I was chosen to attend a 4-H Leader's Conference in Reno, Nevada. My cousin, Ted Gaydon was stationed at Beale Air Force Base in California. Louise and I and Pamela drove out to Reno for the conference. Louise and Pam stayed with Ted's family while I was in Reno. After I returned to the Gaydon home, Vonnie drove us into San

Francisco, toured the town and ate lunch on Fisherman's Warf.

In the early 70's Louise and I bought a used Travel All and a 21 foot pull type camper from her Aunt Violet Sneary. Uncle Jack had passed away and Aunt Violet sold us the whole unit. The International Travel All was roomy but a little more like a big truck to handle.

Several years later we traded the Ford Courier for a used Super Cab Ford Pickup with a nice topper. This gave us a unit with power steering and would fit the camper setup to a T. We put a bed in the topper and the boys thought it was great to ride back there when we went on a trip. They put in a stereo system to listen to while traveling.

In the late 70's we decided to take a long trip to the Pacific Northwest. Rod did not go as he was working full time. We stopped at Salt Lake City and visited some Gaydon cousins and went on to Reno, Nevada and on into California and up the coast to Oregon. We visited the Findleys for several days. We also stopped to visit Alva and Gladys Berry (formerly a Crabtree). We stayed around for several days and Alva showed us around that part of the country. Louise had the honor of staying back to catch up on laundry! We left our trailer at their house and went to Vancouver Island, taking the ferry and pickup over there. We stayed the night there and toured the Bushart Gardens which were spectacular.

We left again with the trailer going to eastern Washington. We spent several days with the Baldwins, who had been neighbors to us in Colorado. Their family and all of us went to the Grand Coulee Dam for a day as it was not far from Ephrata where they lived.

When we left Washington we traveled through Idaho and on to Star Valley Wyoming and stopped briefly at Rayma and Elmer Wofley's home. This was a long trip, but was filled with many great memories and outstanding scenery.

By the early eighties a lot had happened. Rod and Deborah had married in 1979 and moved to Mount Vernon, MO. Our first granddaughter, Catherine Jean was born in 1980, followed by the birth of Levi and Anna while they were still living in Missouri.

Dwight had married his senior year in high school and he and Misty became parents to Kimbra LaNae in 1981. Their son, Jeffrey Scott was born in 1983.

I resigned my position as a letter carrier at the Post Office in 1982 because of health issues. I had started part time pumper work in the oil field and would soon go on full time, pumping oil and gas wells, contracting with several different companies. I was still farming and raising cattle.

Tim and Christie were married in 1990 prior to their deployment to the Persian Gulf. Dwight served in the Desert Shield and Desert Storm with them also. Tim and Christie have two children, Seth Alan, born in 1997 and Taylor Ann, born in 1999. They were both born in Durango, CO.

Our daughter, Pamela Lynn married Jeff Spitzer in April 1992. To this marriage also came Kyle, age four and a half and Eli, age three. Pam proudly adopted Jeff's sons becoming their mother.

In the early nineties I was appointed as officer-in-charge of the Bristol Post Office. The Post Office was closed for good two years later.

I continued working full time for an oil company in 1993. This gave me paid benefits for insurance, sick leave and annual vacation time. I had been working as a contract pumper before this with no benefits. I resigned from the full time position and still fill in part time. The last five years, from 2010 to the present 2014 the part time has been mostly in the summer and fall as we have been going to Arizona in the winter to enjoy the warm weather.

Dwight remarried in September 2006 to Michelle Cook and they are currently living in Laguna Hills, CA. Michelle has a daughter, Heidi, whom we love like a granddaughter.

Tim remarried in October 2006 to Stacy Moore. Stacy has two sons, Quentin, age 17 now and Colin, age 14 now. Tim and Stacy have a daughter, Kayla Susan, born September 14, 2007. She is a lively first grader! They lead busy, active lives with these five grandchildren and the many activities they are involved in.

Louise's Dad, Everett Bever, passed away in June 1982. He was ninety and a half years old. He was born November 20, 1891 in Chautauqua County, Kansas.

My Dad, Dwight Moody Clark, passed away in January, 1994. He would have been ninety six years old on April 5th. He was born April 5, 1898 in Chautauqua County, Kansas. My Mother, Bernice Ruth Keeler Clark, passed away in September, 1997. She would have been ninety three years old on December 7th. She was born December 7, 1904 near Fayettevile, Arkansas.

Louise's Mother, Mary Ellen Kepp Bever passed away in June, 2008 at the age of ninety six and a half years old. She was born December 24, 1911 in Illinois and moved with her family by covered wagon to Arkansas.

The summer before my Mother died in 1997, I had a freak farm accident but did not have any surgery until August 19, one month before Mother's passing. They replaced the bone at the top of my neck with bone from my hip and a titanium plate. With lots of prayers and excellent medical care I healed. I am restricted on how far I can turn my neck each way and up and down but am very fortunate that I am not paralyzed!

Now I feel like it is time to start to close down this part of the story of my life. I will be seventy eight years old this year (2014).

Remember how my story started as an orphan? I will now go back to the beginning and answer the questions I had most of my life, do I have blood relatives and if so, how many?

The Rest of My Story:

Chapter Eleven

It was the latter part of March 2006 that Louise was talking with me about my life. We had these conversations many times. As a young boy around five years old, my Mother had told me that I was adopted. She told me what adoption meant and that I was brought into this world by a young girl who couldn't care for me and wanted a family to adopt me and give me a good home. I remember asking her if I had a name before I was Steven Keith Clark. She told me my last name was Callender and that my birth mother was very young and from northern New Mexico. I remembered that name from that time on, and I also wondered if she had made up that name or if it really was Callender. It was about fifty five years later, probably 1995 at Thanksgiving time when all of our children and their families and Louise and I and Mother were sitting around a cozy fire in the fireplace in the basement talking and telling stories.

Mother got on the subject of how she and Dad added me to their family. She said she and Dad went to Denver in July 1936 and went to an orphanage to look for a child. She said there were lots of children from babies to older ages. She told how they walked through this place and some older children looked up to Mom and Dad and said "take me, take me". She said Dad looked at me and at three months old I smiled at him. Dad said, "that's the one I want right there". That was July 3, 1936.

I never asked or talked to Mother much about the details of my birth, mainly because I thought it might hurt her feelings if I began to pry into my past. Everyone who knew my parents and me know I have a very loving and good life.

I might repeat again that I was told they did not have a name picked out for me but when they got out to the ranch southwest of Lamar that Granddad Clark said name him Steven Keith Clark. You see, Granddad's name was Stephanus and his mother's maiden name was Angeline Keith. My Granddad and Grandmother Clark were very special grandparents as most all grandparents are. They spoiled me very much, partly because I was the grandchild that lived close by. Now back to the day in March 2006 when the conversation turned to the possibility of biological parents, and brothers or sisters.

Louise said we should go to the Prowers County Courthouse in Lamar to see if they have records on my adoption. We went to the District Court office and inquired there. It was late afternoon on a Friday and the clerk took what information I could give her and told me she would call me Monday morning regarding any records she could find. I also had told her that my birthday was April 4, 1936 but our house had burned down when I was five and lost my birth certificate in the fire. Just before my sixteenth birthday I applied for a copy of my birth certificate so I could get a driver's license. When I sent in the request to the State of Colorado the copy came back that my birth date was April 1st.

Monday morning when we arrived at the Court House the clerk who had taken my information asked me if I knew what my name was before I was adopted. I responded with 'I guess it was Callender'. She asked if I knew the rest of my name. I told her I had no idea. She said the records showed it was Herbert Leroy Callender. All this information was found when she searched on the microfilm. She let me look at the microfilm. Here it was 2006 and I was looking at information from 1936 and 1937.

Most of what she told me was that I had been awarded to the State of Colorado by my birth mother at the age of three months. It did not give my mother's name. The film did tell of Dwight and Bernice Clark taking me and it also told of my adoption being applied for the next year and approved on May 21, 1937. May 21st is the birth date of our youngest son, Tim.

It was apparent that my mother had kept me for three months before turning me over to an orphanage. I was there less than a week before being taken by Dwight and Bernice for possible adoption.

I searched on the computer for the name Callender in New Mexico and also Colorado. I took names and addresses and composed a letter and also photos of myself at various ages and also included pictures of our three sons and a short biography of my life. I received around eleven replies and several telephone calls. All wished me well in my search.

One gentleman wrote an amusing response back to me. He knew I was a Callender because my ears stuck out like all Callenders did! His father told him that Callender ears stuck out like a taxi cab going down the road with both doors open! He lived in Pueblo West and was elderly and had been to Scotland and had a Coat of Arms from there. However, I could not be directly tied to his family.

After much thought, I decided to take the advice given to me from the people at the court house, which was to have a judge sign a court order and hire an intermediary to obtain my original birth certificate. This search would also show if I had any biological relatives. The paperwork was filled out at the court house and within ten minutes I had the court order signed by a judge and ready to mail.

Within a week I had a telephone call from a woman in Denver telling me that she had been assigned to my case! After another few days she called and said she found out who my biological father was. She could not give me a name yet as he also had other children from whom she had to get approval. She did say that he was born in 1920.

Another telephone call revealed to me his name was J.W. Sims and he had a son in Wyoming and a daughter in Montana. She had not found any information on my biological mother yet except her last name was Callender and was sixteen years old and J.W. was fifteen years old when I was conceived.

The intermediary said as soon as she cleared it with the brother and sister to consent to my contacting them, she would give me their names and telephone numbers. Consent was given! I called my brother, Ron Sims of Basin, Wyoming and talked to his wife, Barbara. Ron was out playing golf and would be home later. I visited with Barbara and found that Ron and I had similar interests. He was involved in mechanics and also owned a Model A Ford as I did!

When I called my sister, Jan Johnson, in Helena, Montana, she was as excited as I was. She wanted to meet at Ron's place the next week. We waited one more week to make things work out for this meeting. It was hard for all of us to wait but Louise and I drove to Ron and Barbara's house on the outskirts of Basin, Wyoming in June. There was lots of talking and laughing sharing our lives. Jan brought a lot of pictures. I really never thought I would ever find anyone on the father's side, but here I was with a brother and sister. We all had the same father, J.W. Sims but each had a different birth mother! Jan had a picture of J.W. Sims in his army uniform. Louise looked at that picture and cried! She said 'Keith, that is YOU'. It was almost identical to the picture of me in my military uniform in basic training.

The intermediary continued searching for my birth mother. She said New Mexico was really tough to get information from.

In the meantime, our oldest son, Rod and his wife Deborah were busy on their computer with the little information we had. J.W.'s dad, Paschal Sims lived in northern New Mexico near Grenville. In 1935 the drouth was so bad that he rented some grassland for a year between Albuquerque and Santa Fe, New Mexico at Los Cerrillos. He moved his whole family with him. This is where J.W. and and Dorothy Jane Callender became acquainted at school.

Rod and Deborah traced the Callenders to that area and found a Weyman and Belle Callender living there in the early 1900's. A son, Claire Callender was born in 1905 and a daughter, Dorothy Jane Callender was born in 1919. Claire Callender had one daughter, Nedra, who lives with her husband, Larry Gordon in Albuquerque.

We attended a Bever cousin reunion in Corona, CA in June 2006. Driving home from California, we decided to check out the place where J.W. and Jane had evidently met in school. We stopped at the Post Office and I asked the postmistress about perhaps visiting with an older person in town that had lived there for a long time. She referred me to Mary Mora, who was close to ninety years old and owned a Bar there in town. It was close to 10:00 a.m. but I knocked on the rear door and this little Italian lady answered the door. I told her I was doing family ancestry and asked her if she ever knew a Jane Callender. She said 'yes, I had gone to school with her'. I asked if Jane had any children, hoping some might live around there. She looked at me and said Jane never had any children, but then said 'I take that back, she had a boy, but gave him up'! I said, 'Ma'am, you're looking at him'! She invited us in and we had a pleasant visit. She told me quite a bit about Jane, her parents and where they lived and what they did.

I was not supposed to do any searching as that was what the intermediary was hired for. But the intermediary was willing to talk to Rod about his finds.

I contacted Nedra Callender Gordon and she and her husband, Larry, agreed to meet us in Los Cerrillos. Deborah had a business meeting in Santa Fe and after the meeting, she and Rod and Louise and I drove to Los Cerrillos. We met the Gordons at a place where a lot of artifacts were on display from the area. In looking through the owner's collections, we found pictures of Wayman Callender with a baseball team many years earlier. The Gordons showed us where the Callender home had once been. Wayman, along with his father and brother had holdings in the turquoise mine. Some of the old business buildings had Wayman's name on a plate by the door that he at one time had owned these buildings.

We drove over to the town of Madrid about fifteen miles away. Wayman and his brother had constructed houses there at the turn of the century.

I had now made contact with both my mother and father's family. Nedra is my first cousin, her only cousin as she was an only child and Jane had no other children. There may have been a family conflict between Nedra's father and my biological mother so Nedra did not grow up knowing her Aunt. This conflict probably started when Wayman died. We have met a daughter and son of Larry and Nedra's who also reside in Albuquerque.

Ron and Barbara celebrated their 50th wedding anniversary in 2006 but waited until that the fall to celebrate. This was celebrated in Taft, California where they lived for many years when Ron worked in the oil fields. Five of their six children were still living near Taft. Louise and I knew we wanted to go there and also meet their children and grandchildren. We flew there taking our three children from Colorado with us. Rod also took his son, and our grandson, Levi. Dwight and his wife, Michelle and Dwight's son, Jeff, drove up from Laguna Hills. This was the icing on the cake! My sister, Jan Johnson, also flew in from Montana.

A year and a half later, on April 20, 2008 Louise and I celebrated our 50th wedding anniversary. We had a wonderful day, renewing our vows and a catered late lunch with a lot of our wedding party there and then a reception that afternoon. Our children hosted a wonderful day for us. Ron, Barbara and Jan drove to Lamar for this special occasion.

The three of them and Louise and I spent a day driving to Grenville, New Mexico where Ron was born. We went to the ranch house where J.W. lived as a young boy. We also visited the cemetery where a young sister of J.W.'s was buried. She died as a young child.

We traveled to Clayton and ate supper there at an old hotel that had been refurbished. It was a wonderful restoration. We drove on back home and a few days later they left for their respective homes.

Ron had called me when they got home and said they spent the night in Brighton, CO where J.W.'s youngest sister, Ann and her husband, Bill Adams lived. I only knew of them thru the history of the Sims that Jan had put together for me.

One day while we were wintering in Green Valley, AZ for three months, my cell phone rang. It was my Aunt Ann calling. We visited for a long time. I knew right away that we had to meet. She was an aunt to me but only about five months older than me. We traveled to Brighton at our first opportunity after returning from Arizona. We have visited with Ann and Bill several times since that first meeting. They came to our Granddaughter, Kimbra Birchler's home in October 2012 when all of our children were there along with numerous grandchildren and great grandchildren. We found out that the Birchler's and Adams did not live too far apart! We talk to each other every few weeks. I feel very blessed to have met more of my biological family. I knew that I needed to meet Aunt Jenna, Ann's older sister that lived in California.

My brother, Ron Sims, passed away on Thanksgiving Day 2011. A memorial service was held the following May in Taft, California. Tim and I flew to Dwight's in California. Dwight drove us along with his son, Jeff to the memorial service. We had contacted Nadine, Aunt Jenna's daughter about driving to their home in Atascadero, California. They were only 100 miles away from Taft. We had a wonderful visit and a wonderful meal with Aunt Jenna and her daughter and husband, Nadine and John Dorn. Nadine is a first cousin to me. Aunt Jenna was ninety-two years old. She is a beautiful person inside and out. She agreed with Ann that I looked so much like my biological father, J.W. Sims. We took numerous pictures of all of us.

In February 2013 we again drove to California to visit Dwight and Shelly. Louise really wanted to meet my Aunt Jenna but she was in Sacramento visiting a granddaughter. In November 2013, we again went to Dwight and Shelly's and spent ten days at Thanksgiving time. Dwight drove us the two hundred plus miles up to Atascadero again and Louise finally met Aunt Jenna! It was a short visit but Louise agreed that she is a beautiful and loving person.

That is My Story as of this writing. After spending the winter in Arizona, Louise and I are home in Colorado once again and look forward to another spectacular year. We wish you all the best.

Chapter Twelve

These are some of the stories from my years as a Letter Carrier.

On one of my first Sundays to work alone in the Post Office, I had made my afternoon route collection of the town's collection boxes and returned to the Post Office. A contractor would soon be there to pick up the sacks of mail for the train. They were hung on a hook for the catcher to use a pole to retrieve the sack of mail as the train didn't make a complete stop. When I returned to the Post Office the contract carrier was waiting to pick up the mail for the train. I hurriedly went in the Post Office and brought out the mail sacks. The Post Office door automatically closed behind me and locked. I had left the keys inside on the counter! This Sunday afternoon was in the summertime. I drove to where I could use a telephone and called the employee who had worked that morning with me. He said he would be right down to see what could be done. When he arrived he had his son with him who was around four years old. We opened the package drop that was a spring door big enough for small packages. He put his son thru the drop door and told him to go open the door to the Postmaster's office, which also led into the lobby where we were. Problem solved!

In the winter of 1972 and 1973 we had a lot of snow and it was packed on the streets like an ice skating rink all winter. One day as I was walking with my mail bag over my shoulder I saw a Volkswagon coming my way. I knew I had to hurry across the street to get out of the way, but I slipped and fell. I could see the vehicle slipping and sliding toward me. That was the fastest crawl of my life but I got out of the path of the car.

An older patron who lived in Paseo Place was backing her car out of her garage when I was only a few houses from her house. When she saw me she was going to see if she had any mail. She stopped her car in the street and got out to greet me. She failed to take the car out of reverse. I looked up and saw the car going backwards. She was out of the way of the car but I knew she could not catch it. I dropped my mailbag and made a fast run and caught up with the car. However the car going backwards with the driver's door open proved difficult to do. I did manage to get in it and put on the brakes and put the car in park. She was one scared lady. She could not thank me enough!

Another patron who also lived in Paseo Place had a huge cement front porch with a porch swing. In nice weather she could usually be found sitting in the swing watching the neighborhood. She had cement flower pots on each side of the steps up to the porch. They were about the size of a five gallon bucket. This one year before she had planted anything in the pots she noticed something growing in the two biggest pots. She told me she hadn't planted anything in the pots yet but would just let them grow to see what developed. I had looked at some marijuana plants around this time at the police station. I told her they looked to me like marijuana. A few days later when the dozen or more plants were about twelve inches high, both pots disappeared during the night. Evidently whoever planted them in the flower pots knew they were ready for the harvest.

On a very hot day in this same neighborhood I was at a house where the lady occasionally gave me a Dr. Pepper to drink. She gave me one this day. I thanked her and went on down the street about five houses. Mrs. Ausmus (Monte's grandmother) met me at the door with a glass of Coca Cola. She told me as hot as it was I would enjoy it. I drank it and thanked her and went on down the street. Toward the end of the street, about eleven houses away another patron had a big glass of ice water for me! I did not want to hurt her feelings so I drank it. I hoped that was all the good generosity offered to me that day. It was!

Hobo was a two-faced dog! When I delivered the mail on the high porch where the dog lived, he wanted to bite me. I had to be careful that he did not come up behind me, or he would try to bite me. We were friends of the people who lived there and often had Sunday School class parties at their house. If Hobo was in the house, he would always want me to pet and makeover him. But come the next day when I had the mail in my hand it was the snarling and growling of a mean dog. One Valentine's Day I received a card from Hobo. The card read like this: 'Valentine, sometimes I have the DOG gonedest urge to take a bite out of you, be my Valentine'. There was a paw print from Hobo inside the card!

One mail patron always greeted me when I delivered her mail when she saw me walking up to her mail box. One Sunday after church I had stopped at Safeway to get a few groceries. I stood in the checkout line behind her. She did not see me until she was paying for her purchases. She turned around and said 'Keith, I didn't recognize you with your clothes on!' The checker and three or four people behind me were as startled as I was as she stuttered and stammered 'I mean without your uniform on'. Everyone kinda chuckled but I think she and I turned several shades of red.

A young boy named Tommy had a grandpa he called Grandpa Buck who had moved several hundred miles away from Lamar. Tommy was around four years old and was always asking me if he had any mail from Grandpa Buck. He lived on a corner and his parents gave him permission to walk with me to the end of the block. One day Tommy asked if he had a letter from Grandpa Buck and I replied 'No Tommy, maybe tomorrow'. He was quiet during our walk to the other end of the block. When we reached the corner and I was ready to cross the street I said, 'see you tomorrow'. Tommy looked up at me and said 'can I ask you something'? I said 'sure, what'? He replied 'can I have tomorrow's mail now'?

After becoming motorized to deliver the mail, I still enjoyed walking Paseo Place loop by foot. That gave me a little exercise and I did not have to jump in and out of the jeep. One day a young boy just older than Tommy in the previous story was always asking a lot of questions. He sometimes walked the loop with me. One day he wanted to know how old I was and I asked how old did he think I was. He thought I was around seventy. I was probably under forty years old! One time when I was getting back in the jeep to leave he noticed the steering wheel was on the right side. He said 'you know what? Your handlebars are on the wrong side'!

Writers Cramp Publishing

editor@writerscramp.us

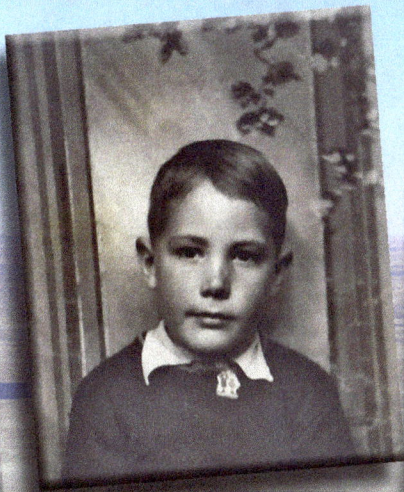

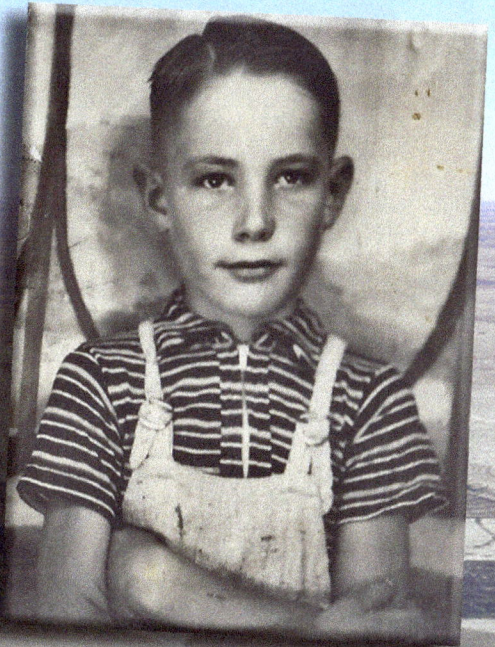

Dating years

Our Wedding, April 20, 1958

Colonel Moynaham with Keith and Louise March 1960

Keith and Louise on our 50th Anniverary, April 20, 2008

Easter Sunday 1970

Keith standing next to half sister Jan Johnson and half brother Ron Sims in 2006

The Clark Family

Keith's 1951 Ford identical to the one he and Louise had when they were married.

Dwight and Bernice Clark on their 50th Anniversary in Keith's 1929 Model A Ford

Grand Children and Great Grand Children: September 2013

Children, Grand Children and Great Grand Children: September 2013

www.ingramcontent.com/pod-product-compliance
Lightning Source LLC
Chambersburg PA
CBHW051956090426
42741CB00008B/1426